RAMAYANA YATRA

A Journey through Sacred Lands

Prabhu Sharma

INDIA • SINGAPORE • MALAYSIA

ISBN

Hardcase 979-8-89610-339-4

Paperback 979-8-89544-899-1

I dedicate this book to my parents,
Father - Pundit Brahama Nand,
and Mother - Savitari Devi.

CONTENTS

PREFACE

In my childhood, I was always fascinated by the stories in The Ramayana, but curious about how it is possible for a human to fly over the ocean like Hanuman did; and how could stones float on the sea? In the 80s, some films and programmes on television about spiritual aspects attracted me. Later, some documentaries about the incidents that took place during the era of The Ramayana inspired me to investigate them discreetly. The idea of writing a book on The Ramayana sites intermittently came up after watching the news about Rama-Lalla – (infant Rama) enshrined under the tent instead of glorifying the temple. Some news channels fanned it more when they showed more places in Sri Lanka related to the epic text.

"The finest things in life are not always easy to achieve; you have to go the extra mile to obtain them." It was certainly the case when I started to research the feasibility of reaching those areas. The dream of viewing those places kept simmering in the back of my mind every time I thought about my vacations.

One day, my wife, Janak, brought a cup of tea when I was shuffling the papers about the sites to explore.

"You can write a book with that many papers," she said while placing the cup on the side of the table.

"That was it."

It laid the foundation stone for the idea of penning down a book as the topic was already bubbling in my mind. I slid my spectacles onto my head and rubbed my left temple while sipping the tea. I thought about it for a good while. It nestled in my mind for many days. It was a marathon of research to discover the sites I wanted to visit and their viability to explore. I mapped out my first itinerary to Nashik and Nepal, but for some reason, I had 5 extra days to travel. Therefore, I initiated my maiden journey from Sri Lanka.

The prayers and teachings of my grandmother have always been the driving force in my smooth life. Hadiabad (Phagwara), where I grew up, may not be related to any incident that occurred during The Ramayana era, but Lord Hanuman's blessings have certainly played a major role in my existence. When my grandmother received the message of my arrival in the world from my maternal grandmother's dwelling in Jagraon, her happiness knew no bounds. She immediately went to Chadha's temple and wholeheartedly begged for my long life before Lord Hanuman. In return, she vowed and committed herself to pray every evening. It was a very emotional moment for her as my parents had lost all 4 children within a week of their birth. She always had great faith in her Lord. She kept her word till she breathed her last in June 1984, the month of my birth. She had walked daily to the shrine barefoot for 31 years, regardless of the severity of the weather or her health. I dedicate every success in life to my grandmother.

After my basic education at the government school in Hadiabad (Phagwara), I stayed with my aunt and uncle in Kartarpur to continue my education. They always cared for me like their own sons. While doing a Commerce Degree from DAV College Jalandhar, my parents arranged my engagement to Janak in England without my ever having met her or communicated with her. I respected their decision as I thought no parent would do anything wrong for their child. I joined Janak in 1977 after completing my Post Graduation in Economics. My father wanted me to be a Lawyer, but I ended up in the United Kingdom selling sports goods, spirits, wines, beers, and general groceries. I have been in the retail business since Christmas Eve, 1977, but bought my independent business in May 1981. I am a non-smoker, vegetarian, and teetotaller despite owning a shop selling nearly everything. Some of my friends call me a 'Walking Dead Man'!! Now, my itineraries were ready; the only way to survive the entire journey was to have 2 strong legs and a spiritual mind!

HOW THE RAMAYANA WAS COMPOSED

The Ramayana is an epic poem which narrates the triumph of virtue over vice and imparts lessons on being an ideal human being. The epic text, The Ramayana - originally written by Valmiki, a Sanskrit poet - contains 18 books and 24,000 verses in 7 *Kandas* - cantos. The Uttra *Kanda* - the *seventh Kanda* - is believed to be a later addition to the original story that concerns the final years of Sita, Rama and his brothers. The Ramayana describes the immortal tale of Rama, which teaches the values of ideology, relationship, duty, and devotion, and it portrays the ideal characters. Valmiki depicts Rama not as a supernatural being but as a human with all the associated shortcomings who encounter moral dilemmas but overcomes those by simply adhering to the *dharma* - the righteous way.

There are 2 forms of literature in Hindu scriptures – Shruti and Smriti. Shruti – the Vedic Literature – includes major Vedas, Upanishads, and Aranyakas, which is ultimate. It cannot be changed. But The Ramayana falls under Smriti. Smriti, literally meaning "that which is remembered," is a body of Hindu texts usually attributed to an author, traditionally written down but constantly revised, such as Puranas and epic texts. We cannot read the Indus Valley Civilisation script, which is over 3000 BCE old, and in the same way, we might not read scripts before that either. The Ramayana was orally transferred from generation to generation, but the timing of the epic texts differed among the intellectuals. Some experts believe that it was written around 500 BCE; some historians think that it was written around 1900 years ago. In fact, Rama belongs to an era when the Prophet

Mohammad and Jesus Christ were not yet born. The Christian, Muslim, and Sikh faiths were then unknown to the world.

According to legend, the poet of The Ramayana was originally a robber. Ratanakar - Valmiki's original name - was very skilled in using swords, bows, and arrows. Sumali, his father, often remarked that Ratanakar was the best warrior he had seen in their clan. When Ratanakar grew up, he had a large family to support. He decided to use his skills and began to rob passers-by.

One day, Ratanakar came across Narada, a Vedic sage who, of course, owned nothing. He was playing his *Tambura* - a mandolin - and singing the praises of his Lord. Ratanakar wondered why any person would come to the forest with a musical instrument. However, Ratanakar eyed the *Tambura*; he thought that the ascetic had hidden his valuables inside the musical instrument and was pretending to be a simple man. Ratanakar slowly pulled out his knife and pointed it at the ascetic.

The ascetic looked amused and asked, "What do you want, son?"

It irritated Ratanakar as the ascetic was not even getting scared of him.

"Give me all your belongings, you old man," Ratanakar said, carelessly waving his knife.

Ratanakar became angry when he saw the ascetic burst out laughing.

"Belongings; do I look like someone who has any valuables?" The ascetic pointed at his *Tambura* and said, "I have this... You can have it if you want."

For the first time, Ratanakar felt uneasy. He yelled to himself, "Why is this man not getting scared of me?"

"Is anybody accompanying you? Are you wandering alone in the jungle?"

The ascetic smiled and said, "I always go everywhere alone... I have my *Narayana* - the Lord - to help me in case of need."

"Who are you?"

"I am Narada, Lord Brahma's son."

Ratanakar was momentarily shaken and asked, "Brahma's son... Who roamed around the Earth and carried messages from all over to the Gods, that Narada?"

"Yes, but do you know that what you are doing is a sin?" Narada said amusingly.

Ratanakar gave an uneasy laugh and said, "So... Who cares? I do what I have to do to feed my family. If I do not rob anybody, my family will starve. I find there is no sin in it."

"Fine, if you feel so," said Narada.

"But, can you go home and ask your family whether they are willing to share the burden of sins you are committing... I promise I shall wait here till you come back."

Ratanakar looked with astonishment at Narada. He felt he had to know the answer before killing him. Ratanakar tied Narada to a tree and hurried to ask his family the same question.

He went home and said to his father, Somali, "I am a thief... I rob, and sometimes, I kill people. I make sure that my family is fed and clothed. I want to know... whether you all will share my sins with me?"

Sumali was astonished. "Share your sins with you," Sumali asked angrily.

"It's your duty to look after your parents when they are old. Why should we share your sins for doing your duty?"

Ratanakar felt as if he had been slapped. He went to his wife and asked the same question. He felt doomed when his wife told him that no one else but he would suffer the consequences of his misdeeds.

Ratanakar rushed back to the place where he had tied Narada. Narada was sitting there praying with his eyes closed. Ratanakar slowly untied the sage and fell to his feet; he asked him for forgiveness.

He sobbed and said to Narada, “Nobody was willing to share my sins as I alone was responsible; I have committed many sins.”

Narada picked up Ratanakar and said, “Once you start repenting for your sins, there is always a way.”

“You mean I can make all sins go away?” Ratanakar asked, with a ray of hope in his eyes.

Narada nodded affirmatively. He said, “There is a great man called Rama who is a God among humanity. Close your eyes and keep chanting the sacred name of God - ‘Rama, Rama’ in the inaudible repetition. It will wipe away your sins.”

“For how long should I repeat the mantra of Rama,” asked Ratanakar.

Narada smiled and said, “Till I come back.”

Ratanakar followed his instructions. Days and nights passed, months came, and years went... Yet Ratanakar never moved from the spot. He meditated to the extent that his body became completely covered by ant-hills; however, Ratanakar never knew about it. After a few years of meditation, ‘Rama, Rama!’ turned into ‘Mara, Mara’ - which means death - when ‘Mara, Mara’ spoken backwards, it sounded like ‘Rama, Rama’.

One day, Sage Narada was passing through the same forest and heard a human voice repeating, ‘Mara, Mara’. Narada stopped and noticed that this was the same place where he had encountered the bandit and advised him to chant Rama’s name. So he removed all the ant-hills near the nests of the termites from his body. Ratanakar had attained the supreme state of a great Sage, the one who is at peace with himself.

Narada told Ratanakar, “Your penance has been declared successful. The Gods bestowed upon you the name Valmiki - one born out of ant-hills.”

Ratanakar, the bandit, became ‘Valmiki’.

Valmiki got up and fell at Sage Narada’s feet.

Valmiki dwelt in an *ashram* on the banks of the river Ganges for years. He had lots of followers who came and went at their will. One day, sage Narada paid a visit to Valmiki's *ashram*. It was a pleasant surprise for Valmiki; he felt privileged. Valmiki duly honoured the sage and asked him some questions about humanity. Narada gladly shared his wealth of knowledge on all aspects of life.

Then, Valmiki asked Narada the question he had wanted all these years, "Sage Narada, who is this Rama? Is there any person in the world who possesses the most illustrious qualities?"

Narada smiled and narrated the '*Sankshepta* Ramayana' – Rama's story in brief - which formed the first *sarga* - base - of Valmiki's Ramayana. Valmiki paid attention to Narada's teachings so intensively that he immersed himself deeply in the story.

The next day, as usual, Valmiki went for his daily ablutions around the Tamsa River along with one of his disciples, Bhardwaja.

While gazing at the river, Valmiki said to Bhardwaja, "When I look at the placid water of this river, it reminds me of the qualities of my hero in the story."

Suddenly, Valmiki heard the sweet chirping of birds. He saw 2 Krouncha birds - Doves - sitting on a branch of a tree in a passionate posture. Valmiki felt very pleased seeing the love birds gleefully tweeting. As he was admiring the creatures, a passing hunter shot the male bird, which at once fell dead on the ground. An arrow had pierced his heart. Seeing her wounded partner in a pool of blood, the female bird squawked and lamented over his dead body. The scream of the distressed bird moved Valmiki's heart so deeply that he instantly uttered a curse on that cruel huntsman. However, that imprecation, the curse, came out in a stream of metrical speech.

"You shall not command any respect in society, and your soul will not rest for a long time because you have shot dead an innocent bird who was engrossed in love."

When Valmiki cursed the hunter in a state of anger, he never knew that within the 32-word verse of cursing, unwittingly, there was a prayer to the Almighty Lord Narayana - commonly known as Lord Vishnu - hidden in it.

It was the first '*Sloka*' - a rhythmic line - in Sanskrit literature. This surprised the sage himself. It was an outburst of his inner voice, motivated by the wishes of Lord Brahma. The sage had turned into a poet.

There is no verification or presentation of any subject in the form of '*Sloka*' before Valmiki.

When the thoughtful sage returned to his hermitage, the supreme God, Brahma, appeared in front of him. He instructed Valmiki to compose the entire Ramayana, as he heard it from Narada, in the same poetic metre that issued from his lips when he cursed the hunter.

Lord Brahma said to him, "You have started the glory of Rama, the incarnation of Narayana, who came to end the tyranny of Ravana."

Lord Brahma also gave Valmiki a boon that he would know Rama's past, present, and future. Saraswati, the Goddess of knowledge, is said to have assured the sage and thoroughly guided him as he penned the events of The Ramayana.

Valmiki complied with the instructions of Lord Brahma and wrote the entire narrative account with dignity. Hence, *sloka* by *sloka*, Valmiki composed the epic text. He rightly named it the 'Ramayana' - the story of Rama's march in search of truth and righteousness.

The literary style, the force, the mellifluous movement of the whole theme of the presentation, and a subtly penetrating undercurrent of moral power in the entire epic of The Ramayana make it an almost unparalleled scripture in the world.

INTRODUCTION

Invariably regarded as one of the world's momentous literary works, The Ramayana has a profound impact on culture, art, family relations, politics, and nationalism in India. It combines the inner bliss of Vedic literature with the outer richness of delightfully heartfelt storytelling. The trail of The Ramayana represents a wonderful example of divine sport displayed by the Lord in human form, such as Rama, an incarnation of Lord Vishnu. Rama came to the Earth to protect the sages and heal the woes of society at large.

Since mythology does not require any proof, it can be modulated into faith for constructive goals. Some myths are created, and some are born out of epic tales of when Gods or goddesses walked the Earth like common people. Nowhere else in the world have these kinds of tales come to life with such vitality as in India, where every other festival and the day of the week is dedicated to some divine beings. As The Ramayana is a quintessential part of every Hindu, most of them have heard the tale of The Ramayana many times over ever since they were in their mother's lap.

I believe my journeys to the locations where all the incidents took place during the period of The Ramayana and the interaction with local inhabitants that I have highlighted in the book would help readers and travellers who are keen to explore the mythological, archaeological, cultural heritage, and historical places, as well as the ancient civilisation.

It would certainly enhance the horizon of students, especially in Europe, who study Hindi or Sanskrit in schools or universities, as the texts are directly or indirectly related to the curriculum. The narrative of The Ramayana is already being taught, though under various names, in schools in many South Asian countries, including Thailand, Myanmar, Indonesia, and Cambodia.

This epic poem, compiled by Sage Valmiki, is composed of rhyming couplets called 'Slokas' - verses. These Slokas are categorised into individual chapters called 'Sargas' wherein a specific event is told. The Sargas are again grouped in chapters of books called 'Kandas'.

The Ramayana is composed of 7 Kandas:

1. Bala Kanda – The Book of Childhood; it begins with the story of King Dashratha and the childhood of Rama, followed by his marriage to Sita.
2. Ayodhya Kanda – Book of Ayodhya; this narrates the preparations of Rama's coronation in the city of Ayodhya, his exile into the forest, and the regency of Bharata.
3. Aranya Kanda – Book of the forest; it depicts the forest life of Rama, Sita, and Lakshmana, and the kidnapping of Sita by the demon Ravana, the king of Lanka.
4. Kishkinda Kanda – Book of the Monkey Kingdom; it depicts Rama's meeting with Hanuman. Rama kills the monkey king, Bali, and makes Bali's younger brother, Sugreeva, the king of Kishkinda instead.
5. Sunder Kanda – The Book of Beauty; it shows the detailed accounts of Hanuman's adventures and his meeting with Sita.
6. Lanka Kanda or Yudha Kanda – Book of war; it sheds light on the battle in Lanka between Rama and Ravana, and their respective armies. It also explains the test of fire by Sita and their victorious return to Ayodhya.
7. Uttara Kanda – The last book describes Sita's exile to the forest again, where she gives birth to Luv and Kush, the twins. Eventually, Rama and Sita reconcile; the twin boys later ascend to the throne of Ayodhya, and Lord Rama makes his final departure to the heavenly abode.

Not long ago, going on holidays was a rare luxury, but in recent years, it is customary to have a vacation as soon as you get a chance; many more people enjoy traversing the Earth, especially to the historical and revered places, particularly in India where tourism in mythological sites has increased many folds. Coincidentally, since the Bharatiya Janata Party came into power at the centre in 2014, the Indian Government has been promoting the 'Ramayana circuit' on a priority basis, including the commencement of The Ramayana Train covering all the main circuits; they are spending a phenomenal amount of money on the basic infrastructure.

Many Europeans are familiar with the Indian Gods and Goddesses in this epic poem, yet some readers who encounter them for the first time may not believe in all the supernatural powers and the mythical folklore as they may have a different viewpoint on religious beliefs. But once they plough into the hidden spiritual truth and authenticity of the related sites, the memories will stay with them forever. The entire trail is so dripping in heritage and cultural riches that once you experience the sites, even on a small segment, you are likely to force yourself to plan another sector before you leave the land.

As the structure of every tour was pivotal to Rama's trail, I had no preconceptions of how far I would travel. After extensive research and rigorous exploration, I realised that the wisest way to traverse the unique sites was to travel in quantity and quality. For an epic of this magnitude, it was impossible to travel chronologically to follow the footsteps of Rama. I planned meticulously to exhaust the entire zone so that I could travel with ease. I carved up the 'trail of The Ramayana' into 7 sectors in India, a loop in Sri Lanka, and a snap tour of the eastern fringe of Nepal.

Divinity is a matter of faith, yet mythology and history signify its existence. I went all out to locate and explore all possible settings - little or large - and indulged myself intensively in every sphere that was related to The Ramayana. My motive was not to inspire a surge of interest in the sites, but as my odysseys progressed, they became an integral part of it. I also learnt that visiting mythical and historical places certainly assists in improving moral values and incorporating discipline.

It's never straightforward to distinguish facts from fiction and history from mythology, and it's hard to establish where history ends and mythology begins. But I am sure my honest endeavour of exploring The Ramayana circuit will transport you to the place which you must have heard of but rarely visited.

Although great cultural and geographical changes have taken place since Valmiki wrote this epic, the names of places mentioned in The Ramayana are still unchanged, including Dankarnya forest, Godavari River, Pampa Sarovar, Kamadgiri Parvat, Mithilapuri in Nepal, and Kelani River in Sri Lanka. After exhausting all my itineraries, I felt that, geographically, the trail of The Ramayana is correct and can still be seen.

Many a time, after a day's extensive touring, back at the hotel, I tried to envisage the lives of Lord Rama, Sita, Lakshmana, and Hanuman during the mythical era. Every time, the incidents took me to a sound slumber. This sort of pleasure I felt during the entire journey.

RAMYANA'S SUMMARY

The Ramayana is a magnum opus that guides to God-realisation, the path to which lies in righteousness. The story is not just about Rama and his attempt to rescue his consort, Sita, but also about family values, loyalty, devotion, and *dharma*. Although the main story revolves around Lord Rama, it begins with people on Earth who suffer from the horror and fear of a powerful demon called Ravana.

Equally, Ravana, the antagonist, was a great devotee of Brahma and Shiva. He had practiced austerities to appease them. Consequently, they granted him immunity from being killed by Gods and *Gandharvas* - heavenly ministers, but Ravana did not think it worthwhile to ask for protection from human beings. Vishnu decided to manifest himself as a human being in the form of Rama to vanquish Ravana.

Dashrath, the King of a mighty kingdom, Kosala, had no children from any of his 3 queens: Kaushalya, Kaikeyi, and Sumitra. The family priest, Sage Vashisht, advised him to perform an elaborate fire sacrifice ceremony to seek the blessings of the Gods.

There was a joyous atmosphere in the palace when God Vishnu manifested himself as the elder son of Kaushalya, named Rama Chandra. Bharat was born to his second wife, Kaikeyi, and the third wife, Sumitra, gave birth to twins Lakshman and Shatrughan.

The princes were around 16 years old when, one day, *Rishi* Vishwamittra came to Ayodhya, the capital city. He requested King Dashrath to send Rama and Lakshman with him to protect the sages from demons and evil spirits.

Sage Vishwamitra gave them the necessary education in arts, weapons, science, and archery. Rama could summon many more deadly weapons through meditation to fight against evil forces.

Just a few miles away, there was another mighty kingdom, Mithila, which was ruled by King Janak. The wise Maharaja had organised a Swayamwara - an ancient custom where the bride chooses her husband from amongst several princes, noblemen, and warriors. He laid down a condition that whoever would lift the 'Bow of Lord Shiva' would qualify to marry his daughter, Sita. As King Janak was the custodian of this ancient bow, Sita used to pick it up with ease while doing some household work as she was no ordinary girl.

Sita is the child of Mother Earth. She was found in the furrow of a field when *Maharaja* Janak was ploughing the land. He picked up the child and adopted her immediately. He was overcome with joy as he had no children. The King regarded the child as a 'miraculous gift of God'; hence, he named her Sita - the Sanskrit name for furrow.

Rishi Vishwamittra received an invitation from the King of Mithila to attend a great fire sacrifice ceremony on the day of the *Swayamwara*. He informed the princes and asked them to attend the great function organised by the King. In fact, the *rishi* had nurtured an idea in his mind to get Rama married to Sita.

Lord Shiva's immensely heavy bow was brought into the courtyard by a dozen warriors. *Swayamwara* began immediately. Most of the warriors, kings, and princes tried their luck but in vain; some of them made lame excuses and left before the function came to a close.

The saintly King Janak looked worried and asked, "Are there no warriors left in the world who could marry my daughter? Is the Earth barren of warriors?"

Lakshman's face turned red in rage, but he kept calm; he respectfully asked his brother to show his mettle. Rama stood up, touched his Guru Vishwamittra's feet, and asked for his permission to lift the bow. Rishi Vishwamittra was delighted in his heart; he blessed Rama by raising his hand. Smiling, Rama went to the stage.

He picked up the mighty bow in a flash and bent it so hard that the shaft of the bow broke in the middle; it snapped in 2 with a loud crash. It roared like thunder and lightning.

King Janak's happiness knew no bounds. He was immensely relieved. Everyone cheered and clapped. Rama lowered his head in respect towards his Guru and King Janak; then, he shyly looked at Sita, who was glowing with happiness.

Speedy messengers were sent to Ayodhya to inform Ram's family about his conquest. King Dashrath and his queens gave their consent and organised a massive wedding party amidst great rejoicings. Dashrath's other 3 sons also tied their knots in the same family. Lakshmana wed Sita's sister Urmila. Bharat and Shatrughan married Sita's cousins Mandavi and Shruti Kirti, daughters of Janak's younger brother, Kushadwaj, respectively.

For the next 12 years, Rama and Sita spent happy days together and shared a joyous life in Ayodhya. As King Dashrath was growing older, he summoned his counsellors and asked for their opinion about crowning Rama as the heir to the throne. The counsellors unanimously welcomed the suggestion and agreed to his resolution.

Dashrath announced his decision and gave orders for the coronation of Rama Chandra the very next day, as that was the most auspicious day. Bharat and Shatrughan had gone to see their maternal grandparents, hence were absent from Ayodhya. There was a wave of happiness all over the kingdom.

A hunchback, Manthra, the wicked maid of Queen Kaikeyi, was not happy with the decision to crown Rama as King. Manthra hatched a plan to hinder Rama's coronation. She initiated this by poisoning Kaikeyi's mind.

She cunningly explained to Kaikeyi, "You must be a fool to rejoice in this decision. *Maharaja* knowingly sent Bharat to his maternal house so that Rama could become a King; you have been deceived. You would be treated like a slave if Rama is anointed as a king; his mother would look down on you. You should increase your status by making Bharat the King, and Rama should be dispatched to the forest."

Kaikeyi was confused. She knew that Rama was the elder son of the chief queen; hence, he would be a king. Now, she began to feel insecure in her heart as she was the youngest of the 3 queens. She grew jealous and distressed.

Manthra reminded Kaikeyi, "A long time ago when Dashrath went to help Indra, who was fighting with the demons in the forest, *Maharaja* was grievously wounded; he would have died without your timely help. You had saved his life by quickly taking his chariot to a safer place when one of the wheels had broken on the battlefield. *Maharaja* was so pleased with your quick reaction that he vowed to grant you 2 boons. You said you would ask for them when you needed 2 favours from him."

Kaikeyi remembered and thought that the time had come to specify those 2 wishes. Now, Kaikeyi was well trapped by the crooked Manthra.

Kaikeyi went to the mourning chamber and feigned anger as well as annoyance. Dashrath went to Kaikeyi's palace to share his happiness with her favourite queen. He was shocked to see her lying on the floor with tangled hair loose and adornment rubbed off. Dashrath quickly gathered his courage and asked the reason for her despair.

Kaikeyi replied, "A few years back, you granted me 2 boons, and the time has come to honour them now. So allow me to mention those boons."

Dashrath tried to convince her to postpone her demands until after the coronation and asked her to celebrate the occasion. This made her angrier. She demanded that he grant the boons now, or she would consume the poison.

"Speak out your wishes; they will be fulfilled," said Dashrath furiously.

She swiftly asked, "My first wish is that Bharat be made King; the second is that Rama should be banished for 14 years in the forest."

Dashrath couldn't believe his ears; he fell unconscious. It took a good while to recover his senses; he just cried out in helpless anger.

Dashrath shouted in a loud voice, "What harm has Rama done to you? He always respected you as a mother. Why do you want to ruin my family?"

Dashrath sobbed aloud and pleaded with tears in his eyes, "I always loved you the most and took you to my bosom; have pity on me; please ask for anything but these boons."

The steadfast Kaikeyi stood firm and refused to budge an inch. She shamelessly said, "You, as a King, would never fall back on your words; you have to grant these boons I crave."

Dashrath never felt so helpless and said, "It would have been better if I had died on the battlefield rather than witnessing this horrifying moment of distrust. I grant you these 2 boons but reject you forever."

He cried in a feeble voice and fell unconscious again.

Morning dawned, and Sumantra, his chief counsellor, came to inform Dashrath that all the necessary preparations had been made for the coronation. Kaikeyi told Sumantra to summon Rama immediately.

Rama was shocked to see his father in that unusual state of mind. He asked Kaikeyi, "Oh, mother, have I done anything wrong? Have I offended anyone? Why does his face look so faded with grief? I would rather die than hurt his heart. What's the matter?"

Kaikeyi feigned as if nothing serious had happened and said, "Don't worry, the King is not grief-stricken; he has something unpleasant to tell you. Some years ago, he offered me 2 boons when I saved his life during the battle with the demons. Now, I have asked him to fulfil his promise."

Kaikeyi told Rama about the 2 boons she hankered after. Rama calmly said, "I shall cheerfully fulfil my father's pledge. His words are my command. Call Bharat swiftly, and I will hasten to the forest today."

The news of Ram's decision to banish to the forest of Dandakya spread like a wildfire. Ram's mother, Kaushalya, wept and cried as this grief was too heavy to bear. Lakshman was annoyed at his father's decision but furious with his stepmother for being so selfish.

Rama told Lakshman pleasantly, "Oh, my brother, I would never sacrifice my principles for the sake of the throne. My father's vows are more soothing than the pleasure of the kingdom. I shall leave the palace today."

Rama asked Sita to stay behind to look after his mother, Kaushalya. But Sita begged to accompany him as she explained a wife's position was always beside her husband in sorrow or happiness. Lakshman also pleaded to go along with them. Rama permitted them to follow him. Lakshman's wife wanted to serve her husband, too, but he requested that she stay behind to look after his father and mother.

Rama and Lakshman walked barefoot towards the palace to bid farewell to the king and his queens who were in a dire state. By the evening, Rama, Sita, and Lakshman took leave of all those who were present in the palace and departed from Ayodhya on a chariot driven by Sumantra.

They spent the first night on the banks of the river Tamsa and then continued their journey to Sharingverpur, where they spent another night under a tree on the banks of the river Ganges.

The pangs of separation from Rama proved unbearable. By the time Sumantra reached Ayodhya, King Dashrath had died.

Sage Vashisht sent messengers speedily to bring Bharat and Shatrughan back to Ayodhya without mentioning anything about the incident. After a few days, when they entered Ayodhya, they realised that something drastic had happened. Bharat rushed to his mother's palace and immediately asked for his father and his brother, Rama. Kaikeyi told him all about Ram's banishment to the forest and Dashrath's demise after Rama's departure.

Bharat could not believe his mother would stoop so low with ill advice from her cunning maid; he was stunned by his mother's course of action.

He annoyingly said, "O evil-hearted mother, do you really think I shall accept this proposition and sit on the throne? This kingdom isn't worth anything to me. The real king of this throne is Rama, only Rama."

Shatrughan wept. He was so angry that he dragged the sick-minded Manthra and wanted to slay her. But Bharat intervened and said, "Our beloved brother would never forgive us for killing an old woman. Kaikeyi's name would be pronounced as a wicked and evil woman and a shameful mother."

When Kaushalya, the chief queen, approached Bharat to tell him that he should rule Ayodhya, Bharat sobbed heavily and fell at her feet. He begged her to forgive his mother and vowed he would never sit on the throne but, instead, he would go to the forest immediately to bring back the real King of that throne. Kaushalya felt emotional, too; she hugged him and blessed him. Before leaving for the jungles of Chitrakoot to search for Rama, Bharat performed the last rites of his father.

Bharat went to the forest and humbly pleaded with Rama to come back for the *throne that their father had given him. But Rama refused to return in honour of his father's promise. Bharat's intuitiveness had made him carry a pair of Padukas - wooden sandals as he wanted to place them on the throne until he returned from exile. Before Bharat took leave, he reminded his brother that if they didn't return when the time of their exile was over, he would end his life by sitting on the pyre.*

After spending 11 years in the forests of Chitrakoot and eliminating evil creatures like dangerous animals and demons, they proceeded towards the south into the forest of Dandakaranya. They happily wandered around the jungle for another 2 years and destroyed evil forces from that area, too.

One day, Surpanakha, a demon, spotted Rama near his hermitage. She was attracted by his charming personality and desired to marry Rama. Surpanakha disguised herself as a beautiful young woman and went to allure him. Rama declined her offer. Then, she tried to seduce Lakshman. He, too, spurned her advances. Surpanakha became angry and started to make abusive remarks about Sita out of jealousy. Lakshman could not control his anger; in rage, he leapt forward like lightning and sliced off her nose.

Thoroughly insulted, Surpanakha went to her brother, Ravana. She agonisingly explained what had taken place. Surpanakha specifically described the beauteous Sita so that he would capture her to take revenge. Ravana's face turned red in anger, and they decided to abduct Sita to teach them a lesson.

Ravana went to his uncle Mareech to seek his help. Mareech, who could change his appearance at will, assumed the shape of a beautiful golden deer to entice Sita. He roamed around her hut to draw Sita's attention. Eventually, he succeeded in alluring her towards him. Sita pleaded with Rama to capture the beautiful creature.

Rama told Lakshman to look after Sita until he came back. Rama rushed and followed the track made by the deer. Soon after, Rama pierced the heart of the animal with a divine arrow. The golden deer, in agony, reverted to its original shape and, with his dying breath, cried out in imitation of Ram's voice, 'Help! Lakshman, help'. Rama immediately perceived that he had killed the demon Mareech and suspected something malicious.

Sita, hearing Ram's voice, implored Lakshman to go and see his brother. Lakshman told her that it was an illusion and suspected foul play. Sita was annoyed; she provoked him into leaving.

Before leaving, Lakshman drew a magical protective line, popularly known as Lakshman-rekha, around the hut and said, "You'll be safe if you do not step outside this invisible line. If anybody tries to cross from outside, he will perish in the fire."

Ravana watched it from a distance. As soon as Lakshman left the place, Ravana appeared in disguise as a hermit, begging for alms. Sita went into the hermitage and brought some food and fruits for the holy man. However, he refused to take the alms unless she came out of the open yard. She requested him to come over and pick up his desired articles. This angered the Brahmana, and he threatened to curse her husband if he went away empty-handed. Sita, in fear of her husband's life, crossed the line to hand over the articles. The moment Sita stepped outside the protective circle, the Brahmana suddenly changed back to his original form.

He told her, "I'm not a hermit, but Ravana, the ruler of the demon kingdom called Lanka."

When Ravana dragged Sita by the hair, Jatayu, the King of vultures and a childhood friend of King Dashrath, heard Sita's cries. Jatayu attacked Ravana in a desperate bid to rescue her, but Ravana chopped off his wings, and Jatayu plunged fatally to the ground. Ravana immediately grabbed Sita and carried her into a flying chariot, and he soared through the air to his kingdom.

While all this was happening, Rama was surprised to see Lakshman in the jungle. Rama feared the worst when Lakshman told him about what had happened. They immediately ran back to the cottage and found it deserted. Rama was very upset and heartbroken. Lakshman was in tears; he blamed himself for the abduction.

Rama and Lakshman went southbound in search of the monkey king Sugreeva and Hanuman, who would help in their search for Sita. On their way south, they met an ascetic, Shabri, who had been waiting for years for the sight of her Lord Rama.

After Shabri's deliberation, they went further in search of Sugreeva. Some of Sugreeva's spies rushed to their king and informed him that the 2 men were dressed in ascetic clothes but carrying weapons. Worried, Sugreeva sent Hanuman to verify the news as he thought his brother Bali might have sent these men to spy on his kingdom.

Hanuman changed his appearance to that of a Brahmana and went to see the princes. Upon discovering the identity of those men, Hanuman was overjoyed to meet his Lord but felt sad that he couldn't recognise him at first sight.

Rama related the story of their exile and Sita's abduction to Sugreeva. He vowed to help Rama accomplish his mission of rescuing Sita if Rama could help him fight against the oppression of his rogue half-brother, Bali, who had taken away his wife, Tara, and the kingdom. Rama readily agreed and killed Bali.

The monsoon arrived with a vengeance; Rama and Lakshman decided to live in the cave on Malyavanta Mountain. After the rainy season, Sugreeva summoned a king of bears, Jambavant. Sugreeva sent search parties to all 4 directions. Hanuman and Angad, who led the southern party, discovered Sampati - a vulture, the brother of Jatayu, in the jungle. Sampati, being a vulture with limitless vision, was still able to see clearly over long distances. He told Hanuman that he had seen Ravana taking Sita to Lanka.

Hanuman resolved to visit the island kingdom. Rama felt in his heart that Hanuman would be successful in this mission, so he entrusted Hanuman with his personal ring that Sita would recognise.

Hanuman assumed a gigantic form and swiftly launched himself over the sea. He wandered and searched all around the city and in the palace of Ravana, but Sita was not to be found anywhere.

While searching for Sita, Hanuman saw a Tulsi plant called basil, which is worshipped by Hindus. This was Vibhishan's, Ravan's brother's, house. Vibhishana, who was a devotee of Rama, greeted Hanuman and enquired about his identity. When Hanuman narrated the tale of Lord Rama, they embraced each other. Vibhishana knew that Sita was living at Ashoka-Vatika but was not allowed to enter the garden. Hence, he devised a plan.

Hanuman transformed himself into a dwarf and reached Ashoka-Vatika. At first glance, a thrill of joy passed through his frame as he reached the spot where Sita was captive as a prisoner. Hanuman felt very happy when he saw Mata Sita. Hanuman hid himself among the branches of a tree from the demon servants and waited for the right opportunity to meet her.

The next morning, Ravana came to Ashoka-Vatika, accompanied by his queen, Mandodari, and many other women servants. Ravana approached Sita, still hoping to obtain her consent. He again expressed his desire for Sita and tried every trick in the book to allure her. Sita rejected Ravana's proposal outright. He gave Sita one month to yield to him, or she would face certain death.

Hanuman, while sitting hidden between the branches of the tree, watched all that happened in the grove. Hanuman uttered 'Jai Sita-Ram' and jumped out of the tree; he stood before her with folded hands and bowed his head in salutation.

Sita thought this could be another ploy by Ravana to deceive her. She looked at this strange monkey and asked him, "Who are you? I have never seen you with my Lord. How can I believe that my Lord has sent you?"

Hanuman quickly presented the ring given by Lord Rama and said, "All the demons will be killed by Lord Rama very soon."

But Sita wasn't convinced about Hanuman's capabilities as he had appeared as a dwarf. She thought about how a small monkey like him could fight the mighty demons. When Hanuman showed his real giant form, all her doubts were removed.

Hanuman saw many trees laden with fruits in Vatika. To test the strength of the defences of Ravan's army, Hanuman asked Sita's permission to taste some fruits. Sita duly allowed it but warned him about the demons guarding the Vatika.

Hanuman ate a large variety of fruits while uprooting many trees. Hanuman began tearing his way through the domain of the towers. He killed hordes of demons, whereas some of them ran to the royal chamber of Ravana to inform about how 'a mischievous monkey' caused havoc in Ashoka-Vatika.

Ravana was surprised to hear that an ordinary monkey single-handedly beat up his powerful men. He, therefore, sent his son Akshay Kumar along with a huge army to kill the monkey. Akshay Kumar fought skilfully against Hanuman but was no match for Hanuman's sheer strength; hence, he was killed.

After this sad news, Ravana instructed Indrajeet, his elder son, to capture the monkey and bring him to the royal court so that he could see the creature that had created so much havoc. Indrajeet was such a great warrior that he could rival Rama with his excellent fighting skills.

Hanuman took him on, and they were engaged in a fierce fight. Consequently, Indrajeet captured Hanuman with his illusionary powers and took him to Ravan's court.

Hanuman said to Ravana, "You must release Sita without any delay. It is in the interest of your subjects to send her a respectful message. Otherwise, the punishment Rama bestows upon you will be one of total annihilation."

Ravana was furious that a monkey, in the name of Rama, had the audacity to threaten him, and that too in his own court. He immediately ordered his ministers to kill Hanuman on the spot.

At this juncture, Vibhishana, the younger brother of Ravana, rose from his seat and pleaded, "According to the code of conduct, Hanuman, as an envoy, cannot be killed."

These suggestions angered Ravana even more. Ravana couldn't tolerate this kind of treason from his brother, so he renounced him and forcefully banished him from Lanka.

Now, Ravana thought that monkeys always loved their tails, so he ordered to torture Hanuman by having his tail wrapped in oil-soaked cloth and set it on fire. With his tail burning, Hanuman hopped from house top to housetop, setting Lanka on fire, and caused lots of destruction before jumping into the sea to douse the flames. Hanuman hastened to meet Rama to tell him the news of his loved one. Rama rejoiced and set the ball rolling to cross the sea as soon as possible.

Even though Vibhishana was a demon, he always chanted the name of Lord Rama in the hope of meeting him. So, he crossed the sea and proceeded to meet Rama. When the monkeys in Rama's camp saw Vibhishana coming, they thought a spy from the enemy's camp had come over. They stopped him outside the boundary and informed Rama and Sugreeva.

Although Sugreeva had some apprehensions in his mind regarding the real motives of Vibhishana, Rama explained to him, "It is my vow to protect anybody who takes my refuge. Even if Ravana has sent him to know our secrets, Lakshman can annihilate all ill-minded demons in no time."

Vibhishana explained the incidents that took place in Lanka and said with folded hands, "I have come to seek your refuge and shall serve you sincerely."

Nala and Nila, the celestial engineers, were immediately summoned to construct the causeway between the mainland and Lanka. The entire army of apes and bears constructed a large floating bridge known as Rama Setu or Adam's Bridge; they all crossed the ocean.

Ram's army attacked the fort from all sides. Ravana ordered his forces to kill all the monkeys and bears in the army.

Rama killed Ravan's mighty brother, Kumbhakarn. Indrajeet consoled his father and assured him that the next day's battle would bring death and destruction to Rama's camp.

Indrajeet wanted to kill the duo to avenge the death of his brothers and uncle, Kumbhakarn. He fought fiercely as he could rival Rama with great fighting skills but, for some reason, couldn't hit them directly with his weaponry.

Indrajeet realised that Lakshman couldn't be won over after trying all the weapons. Ultimately, out of frustration and anger, Indrajeet shot his deadliest weapon, Brahmastra, at Lakshman. And indeed, the missile hit him with tremendous force; even the powerful Hanuman was put off balance. Lakshman was uprooted and fell unconscious on the ground, grievously wounded, poised to die.

Terrified, Hanuman rushed to Rama and narrated the whole incident. Rama and Vibhishana were worried about Lakshman's injury. Vibhishana guided Hanuman to bring Sushena, the Royal physician, from his house.

Sushena said, "Lakshman is in a deep coma. You must bring Sanjeevani Booti to cure his wounds. It is a life-saving herb that grows on the Gandhamadhana Hill, located near Kailash Parbat - Mountain in the Himalayas."

Rama looked at Hanuman and instructed him to leave immediately to bring the specified herb before daybreak. Hanuman, the son of the wind, lifted himself in the air and flew faster than the wind.

Hanuman found the mountain, but, to his dismay, he noticed numerous plants adorning the hill; therefore, he couldn't recognise the herb needed for the medicine. Undaunted, he tore up the entire mountain after reciting the name of Rama and began his journey back to Lanka.

Sushena quickly discovered the herb and applied it to Lakshman's wounds. He came back to health, rose up, and asked Ram's permission to fight as before. This resurrection of Lakshman pleased everybody in the camp. Rama patted Hanuman's back and hugged him.

Finally, the frightful war started between Indrajeet and Lakshman. He fiercely fought Lakshman with all his skill in both warfare and sorcery, but Lakshman was unstoppable. Lakshman, who had been waiting to avenge Indrajeet's previous deception, unerringly shot an arrow, Indrastra, which Lord Indra had given him. Indrajeet fell into a pool of blood.

When Ravana learnt about the death of his brave son, he fainted. The exuberant mood in Ram's camp contrasted sharply with the gloom in Ravana's fort. Mandodari wailed uncontrollably. With the fall of Indrajeet, Ravana's spirit was completely in despair, but sorrows soon gave way to anger.

Initially, Ravana had refused to take Rama seriously as he thought that no human being could pose any threat to him. Ravana went to the battlefield in his well-equipped chariot. The 2 huge armies arranged themselves in special formations, where the sound of conches and trumpets generated terror in the hearts of the opponents.

In the battlefield, Ravana and his brave forces created havoc among monkeys and bears. Vibhishana, Sugreeva, and Angad came forward to protect their army. A fierce fight took place between the forces of Ravana and Ram's army.

Rama wasted no time in coming forward and challenged Ravana himself. Following a fierce fight, Ravana's chariot was smashed, and he was severely wounded. Ravana stood helplessly before Rama, whereupon Rama took pity on him and said, "Go and rest now; return tomorrow to resume your fight."

The next day, the battle resumed; Ravana was getting restless. Rama and Ravana hurled missiles at each other, but both were able to counter their opponent's attacks. Lakshman then cleverly killed the charioteer of Ravana, and consequently, Ravana was severely wounded. He fell down unconscious, but another charioteer carried him to a safe place. Rama realised that he had underestimated the strength of the enemy.

The ultimate battle between Rama and Ravana began: Rama severed Ravana's head several times with his arrows, but each time, a new head replaced the severed head. It is believed that Ravana had 10 heads, which he obtained as a boon for his rigorous worship of Lord Shiva. Lakshman, Hanuman, and Angad all tried their missiles on mighty Ravana, but they all proved unproductive. At dusk, both armies retreated to their respective camps.

Rama, Lakshman and their associates were discussing the strategy to put an end to Ravana. After deep thought, Vibhishana recalled how he had faintly overheard a conversation in the family in his childhood about the weakness in the body of his brother, Ravana. The weak spot was his umbilicus - middle abdominal region - where his immortality lay in the Amrit-kunda - life-sustaining nectar.

Vibhishana said, "If Rama could hit the arrowhead in his navel, the life-sustaining nectar would dry up, and Ravana would certainly die."

It is believed that Ravana performed an intense penance to Lord Brahma. Eventually, the creator of the universe, Lord Brahma, pleased with his austerity, offered him a boon. Ravana asked for immortality, which Brahma refused to give, but he was given the celestial nectar of immortality. The nectar of immortality, stored under his navel, dictated that he could not vanish for as long as it lasted.

The next morning, armed with a special weapon and knowledge, Rama drew his bow, Sarang, and shot his final weapon, given by Saint Agastya, the 'Brahmasthra', hurling towards Ravan's navel. Though Ravana had sought invincibility and could replace his head with another, he had never thought of safeguarding his navel. Roaring in agony, Ravana, the mighty king, fell ponderously upon the ground. His torso fell on the ground with such a thud that it caused intense tremors in the Earth.

Severely injured, Ravana was counting his last breaths. Lord Rama said to his brother, "Lakshman, go and approach Ravana for his advice before he dies, as there is nobody else on Earth who could match the calibre of his knowledge of Vedas, Puranas, and ancient scriptures; he is a great Brahman scholar and the most learnt teacher."

Ravana, who refused to chant the name of Rama, recognised Ram's divine identity after being fatally wounded by him; he realised the value of righteousness. When Lakshman went back to Ravana, he gave many useful tips on diplomacy, politics, and statesmanship, etc.

Ravana also told him, "Aaj ka kaam kaal pey matt chhorro," meaning don't leave today's work till tomorrow. Ravana said this in the context of an incident when he stood helplessly in front of Rama, and he let Ravana go from the battlefield and asked him to come back tomorrow.

In the meantime, Mandodari came running to her fatally injured husband with eyes full of tears and a heart filled with unexplainable pathos. All the men and women in Lanka came wailing and crying in grief.

When Vibhishana saw the people of his clan in grief, he became sad. Rama immediately instructed Lakshman to console him. Rama asked Vibhishana to perform the last rites, befitting the grandeur of a Brahman King.

Anyhow, as Rama was still in exile, he couldn't be a part of any merriment; hence, he advised Lakshman to take Sugreeva and Hanuman along with him to the palace to anoint Vibhishana as the new king of Lanka.

Everyone in Ram's camp was eager to seek the blessings of Sita. Joyous Sita, with tears in her eyes, touched Ram's feet. He lifted Sita with tender love.

Rama said to Sita in a soft voice, "As you have lived under the shelter of another man, being a King, I am answerable to my subjects. Therefore, I would like you to undergo an Agni-Priksha - a test of fire - to prove your chastity, though I know your purity is at its highest."

Rama asked Lakshman to prepare a fire-pit for Sita where she would go in the flames. It shocked everyone. A huge fire was ignited, with flames reaching high in the sky. Sita, undaunted, entered the raging flames. Soon, the raging flames in the fire-pit reduced themselves to ashes, and Sita, radiant with satisfaction, was standing in the middle.

Bharat was already waiting for his brothers and sister-in-law to arrive in Nandigram. He was overjoyed to meet Rama, and he laid the 'Padukas' at his feet. Rama happily accepted his gesture. They marched towards Ayodhya, where they were greeted with joy by all his subjects. The entire city was decorated with flowers and streamers; every house was illuminated with rows of earthen lamps. Sweets and gifts were distributed to everyone; there was happiness all around the kingdom. Hence, Diwali, the festival of lights, originated. Rama and Sita were anointed as the worthy King and Queen of Ayodhya.

Rama initiated a long period of just and harmonious Rama Rajya; he had settled down with Sita to rule pleasantly in peace and prosperity. But Sita's sorrows didn't end there. The rumours of her infidelity with Ravana were spreading among the population of Ayodhya. Once a self-indulgent 'Dhobi' - a washerman, Rajak, while beating up his wife who had gone to her parent's house without his permission, shouted in public that he wasn't timid like Rama who would accept his wife back after she had lived for months at somebody else's place. Unfortunately, this comment of the dhobi was reported back to Rama, who very well knew that these accusations were baseless. Nevertheless, Rama wouldn't let slander undermine his rule of kingly dharma.

So, Rama asked Lakshman to banish Sita to the forest for the second time. Lakshman had to obey the king's orders. But Sita wasn't alone this time. She was pregnant with Ram's twins. She was very much hurt by the accusations but was willing to obey the orders of her Lord. Lakshman took her near the hermitage of Sage Valmiki.

Sage Valmiki saw Sita crying and alone. As Valmiki had the ability to see the past, present, and future, he visualised all that had taken place. He took her to his hermitage to stay in the women's wing where Sita gave birth to 2 beautiful sons who were named Luv and Kush. They became pupils of Sage Valmiki, where they grew up to be valiant and intelligent.

Later, when Rama decided to perform a horse sacrifice, he invited lots of kings and princes to attend that ceremony. Sita's twins used to roam around all over the country, singing the whole story of Ramayana during some functions. This was taught by the Sage Valmiki. One evening, they were in Ayodhya; they sang the whole story of Ramayana at the assembly of some prominent people. The people of Ayodhya were astonished, and the news of those boys was conveyed to the King. Rama invited the twins to his chamber and asked them to sing the same story. When they recited the whole story to Rama, he realised that this was his own story.

He asked them, "Who are you, and who are your parents?"

Luv said, "Our mother's name is Sita, and we never asked her about our father."

Rama realised they were his own sons who had been sheltered by their mother in the ashram of Valmiki. He emotionally embraced them and told them their identity.

Rama sent his messenger to his beloved queen, intending to take her back. Rama requested that Sita give proof of chastity to clear her name once and for all, as she has been staying away.

Distress or even humiliation didn't make an impact on Sita. She always obeyed the orders of her Lord. Once again, she bowed to all her elders and was ready to give proof of her purity.

She requested Mother Earth, "If I am truly pure and have thoughts of nobody else other than my Lord, then, O Mother Earth, reaccept me."

Hearing the plea of her pious child and to release her from an unjust world, Mother Earth dramatically yawned and split open into 2 sections. It took her child, Sita, away to a better world.

Everyone was sad after Sita had left the world. Lord Rama was so upset that he threatened to create a powerful deluge and destroy the world if Earth didn't open. Lord Brahma, the creator of the world, reminded him that he was Lord Vishnu; he had accomplished his work on Earth and would surely meet her again in his eternal abode.

Apparently, Rama ruled for the remainder of Treta Yug (the second of the 4 sets of periods) with the highest standards of dharma and divided his kingdom among his family wisely and fairly.

One day, a sage appeared in the palace and requested to meet Rama in a confidential manner. The sage made it clear to Rama that if anybody would listen or see them conversing, he would be sentenced to death. Lord Rama deliberately summoned Lakshman for this task to send him to his eternal abode as his duties on the Earth had been accomplished. Thus, Lakshman sat outside the room as a guard so that nobody could enter the place without his permission.

The sage, in fact, was a Yama Raja - God of Death. He said to Lord Rama, "You, as an Avatar, have completed your earthly duties; hence you are requested to return to your eternal abode."

In the meantime, Sage Durvasa entered the vicinity; he wanted to meet Lord Rama immediately, but Lakshman stopped him outside the room. It made Sage Durvasa very angry. Enraged, Durvasa threatened to curse Ayodhya and Lakshman's entire family. Lakshman, being the Lord Ananta Shesha (Lord of serpents), also knew all about the arrangements for him to go back to his abode. He opened the door where Lord Rama was having a conversation with Yama Raja. Rama had no choice but to send Lakshman to the ocean, where he changed back to his original form, Ananta Shesha. Thus, Lakshman was the first one to leave the Earth.

Eventually, Lord Rama finalised his return after concluding some important tasks: he asked Vibhishana to stay on Earth to worship Lord Jagan Natha. Finally, Rama requested Hanuman to stay on Earth until Kaal Yug - the present time. Rama, along with Bharat and Shatrughan, went to the river Sarayu where they changed their forms for the final journey.

Gate to Rama Temple on the Eve of Diwali 2023

Prabhu at Hanuman Garhi Temple

Kanak Bhawan

Blessings with holy water from Bharat Koop in Nandigram.

Shiva Lingam in Nageshwar Temple

Boating on the Mandakini River

Boating on the Mandakini River in Chitrakoot

Where Bharat asked Rama to return to Ayodhya.

Janak loves to feed monkeys.

Ashok, Shashi, Indu, and Tripta are finding solace from the sun

Temple Tops Across the River

Sunrise from the Hanuman Temple

View of Bali Parvat from Chintamani

Janaki Dham Temple in Nepal

Locals explaining the importance of the place.

Sita Mata Returning to Mother Earth in Sita Marhi

AYODHYA DHAM

When the name of Lord Rama comes to my mind, I am instantly transported to the city of Ayodhya. When the reference to Ayodhya is made, the newly built temple of Rama-Lalla (the infant Rama), where he was born, springs up in front of my eyes. As Ayodhya is the setting and focal point for the great epic poem 'The Ramayana', it is the most reverential sector that infuses oxygen into the soul of the entire trail. It symbolises inner peace and spiritual uplifting. The city is known to every Hindu, even if they do not know its exact geographical location. As Bethlehem is to Christians, so is Ayodhya to Hindus. The cities of Ayutthaya in Thailand and Yogyakarta in Indonesia are named after Ayodhya.

After the extensive tour of Varanasi, we checked into our hotel. On the maiden journey to Ayodhya, I was in a spiritual mood from the moment I set foot on the soil of Lord Rama's birthplace.

The manager of the hotel arranged an auto-driver, Mr Rakesh Pandey, also known as Babloo, for a day. He proved to be an asset as a guide every time I completed part of my tour. He suggested that we visit the Rama-Lalla temple as there were few pilgrims around. There was nothing more elating than visiting the prime site where a small makeshift temple representing Rama as a child was erected.

At times, Babloo threaded maniacally between pilgrims walking in any direction and two-wheelers to reach the site before closing time.

I said to Ashok, "The driver has mentioned that the crowd is quite thin in Rama's temple. The Lord must have known that I am claustrophobic. Generally, there are long queues, and the pilgrims move at a turtle's pace in the congested pathway towards the Rama-Lalla temple."

"Sure, it is a good omen," Ashok said in excitement.

Ramkot, where the Rama-Lalla temple is situated, is the major and foremost place of worship. It is the site of the ancient citadel of Ramkot, which stands on elevated ground in the western part of Ayodhya. The compound was surrounded by high steel fences and heavily guarded by commandos who searched all pilgrims thoroughly before allowing them to enter the site. At that time, the idols of Sita, Lord Rama, and his brothers, along with Hanuman, were adorning the shrine in the tent.

As we reached near to the temple vicinity, Babloo reminded us that no possessions, including mobiles, purses, watches, etc., were allowed to be taken into the temple premises. So, we had no choice but to leave the valuables with Babloo's aunt, who had a souvenir stall nearby.

By the time we reached the first checkpoint, the crowd was a lot thinner. We ambled through the road that led to the main entry point of the long pathway to the shrine. The security was so stringent that even a sweet in my mouth was not allowed to be sucked. I lost a strawberry-flavoured candy!

It did not take long to figure out the spot where Lord Rama was born. A small crowd was gathered at the barricade opposite the shrine. I was brimming with excitement. Generally, they would not allow anyone to hang around for long, but by the grace of Lord Rama, I was rewarded with a clear view of the idols. Although the idol of Lord Rama in a standing posture was around 7 metres away, I still felt so near to him. The soothing sound of Rama's prayers made the atmosphere more spiritual.

I made way for other devotees to pass by, clinging to the metal fence while talking to the priest and getting the prasad. I constantly cherished the view of the shrine for a bit longer and enjoyed the atmosphere. I felt a great sense of exhilaration.

BIRTH OF LORD RAMA

The building of the Rama Temple at the place of his birth is the pinnacle of events in this yuga, especially for Hindus. Lord Rama was born on the ninth day of the increasing phase of the moon in the lunar month of Chaitra. It is believed to be on the 10th of January, 5114 BCE, at 12.30 pm. The *family Guru of the Raghu dynasty, Sage Vashishat, named the Lord, Rama. The name Rama is made of 2 words: Beeja Akharas – alphabetical seeds. The Agni (fire) Beeja – Ra and Amrita (nectar) Beeja – Ma, where Agni Beeja energises the soul, mind, and body, and Amrita Beeja reinvigorates the Prana Shakti – life force – in the whole body.*

HISTORY OF AYODHYA

The word 'Ayodhya' means 'that which is not to be fought' or invincible. This meaning is attested by the 'Atharva-Veda' - religious scriptures - which used it to refer to the unconquerable city of Gods. According to ancient legends mentioned in Puranas, Manu, the progenitor of mankind, founded the city of Ayodhya and gave it to Ikshvaku to rule.

Valmiki's Ramayana centres its tale on a city called Ayodhya, the capital city of the ancient kingdom of Kosala. It was ruled by King Dashrath, who is said to have been the descendant of Ikshvaku. A persistent local fable has it that Ayodhya became desolate after Rama's ascent to his heavenly abode, and King Vikramaditya of Ujjain revived it around 50 BCE. However, Kalidas, a famous poet, narrated in his book 'Raghuvansa' that Rama's son Kusha revived it.

Though the city was known as Ayodhya in Pali language and Ayodhya in Sanskrit during the era of Lord Buddha, its current name was probably established in the 6th century CE. During the Mughal reign, it was the seat of the Governor of Awadh. Ayodhya was annexed in 1856 by the British rulers, and it was part of the United Provinces of Agra and Awadh.

Under Mughal rule, the temple of Lord Rama was demolished, and the Babri mosque was constructed. In the 1850s, a group of Hindus attacked the Babri mosque on the grounds that it was built over the 'birthplace of Lord Rama'. To prevent further disputes, the British administration divided the mosque's premises between Hindus and Muslims.

A movement was launched by the Vishwa Hindu Parishad Party to reclaim the Babri mosque site for a Rama Temple. In 1992, a group of Hindus demolished the disputed structure. Consequently, under the control of the central government, no one was permitted near the site, around an area of 182 metres, and the gate was locked to the outside world.

In 2003, The Archaeological Survey of India (ASI) carried out an excavation at the mosque site to determine if it was built over the ruins of a temple. The excavation uncovered a variety of objects, including a 3.7-metre statue of Lord Hanuman and coins dating to early historical times, along with many other historical objects. The ASI concluded that an ancient temple had been demolished or modified to create the Babri mosque under King Babur.

HANUMAN GARHI

I set the alarm for 5 am and collapsed between the sheets by 9.30. Even then, I kept opening my eyes every hour to check the time. I could not switch off the engines completely. Then, around 4 am, I fell into a deep, dreamless sleep. When the alarm went off, I felt like throwing away the clock and the itinerary for the day. It felt like I had spent most of the night in a state of disturbed wakefulness. Soon after, I woke up to pealing bells just after 5.30 am. Believe me, after wiping the sleep from my eyes, my energy level shot up. I was ready to cherish the early morning spirit of the city.

I decided to start the day with the blessings of Lord Hanuman. As I strolled down the narrow road towards Hanuman Garhi, every shrine on the way was so lively in the praise of Lord Rama that I stopped at almost every setting and admired the atmosphere. I had a strange sense of cheerfulness. It felt as if the incensed fresh air was telling a story of Rama at every step.

As I reached the base of the steps to Hanuman's temple, I bought some Ladoo and a garland of marigolds as my offerings to the Lord. The fragrance of fresh marigold in the morning that wafted from within was unmatched. I looked up at the gate of the temple, bowed, and began to climb a flight of 76 stone steps.

Hanuman Garhi is situated in the centre of the town, standing on elevated ground. The grand configuration of the temple is in the shape of a four-sided fort. Each of its corners has circular bastions housing a small temple of Hanuman. Legend has it that Hanuman lived here in the cave and guarded Ramkot - Rama's birthplace. A small statue of Anjani, the mother of Hanuman, holding the infant Hanuman in her lap, is adorned in the principal temple. It is the most popular shrine in Ayodhya. It is believed that one should visit this temple before praying at Rama-Lalla.

The steps did not feel strenuous as my mind was engaged in the hope of seeing the clear vision of the deities. I could hear the prayers halfway to the cave temple. The common features of the sanctum were the utterances of 'Jai Hanuman' and 'Jai Bajrang Bali' - another popular name for Hanuman. Everyone appeared to register their presence by just looking at the deities that were adorned with red outfits, although most of the faces were covered with marigolds.

Only the beginning of the Hanuman Chalisa broke my vision of the Lord for a split second, and I became a part of the prayers. I felt pleased with myself when I realised that my humming of the Chalisa was audible and synced with other devotees. I jolted my way to the front of the shrine and forwarded the offerings to the priest in a frenzy of chanting and the loud sounds of the bell ringing.

After a couple of minutes, the priest came up and gave me 2 large garlands and lots of Ladoo in return as prasad. I could not hold them in my hands; therefore, I spread out the lower part of my shirt and accepted them with great pleasure. It was a deeply spiritual moment; I felt as if the Lord himself had blessed me with an abundance of happiness. Then, the priest asked me if I could join him in his dwelling that was halfway down the steps on the left. It was like another dose of blessings. I followed him.

It was a small but clean room. The priest and other residents made me feel special. He invited me to join him for a special puja in the temple and a subsequent feast of the offerings at his place the next day. It was a rare privilege when one of the main priests invited me to his ashram. I was thrilled as I knew that I would be able to grasp some more facts and history. I was so excited that I accepted the invitation without realising that I would not be able to make it, as I had already arranged to leave for Lucknow early in the morning. Sadly, I lost a golden opportunity.

Furthermore, I could not visit India for more than 7 years. I realised the sheer power of the Lord, and I sincerely apologised.

When I returned to Hanuman Garhi after 7 years, the place looked very different. A wide road leading to the base of the temple with an identical set up of shops and shutters with selective religious temples in the same colour looked fabulous.

We bought some offerings, including a couple of marigold garlands, before proceeding to the shrine. Janak and I bowed to Lord Hanuman from the base of the temple and climbed the 76 steps with full enthusiasm. It was quite busy, but not as much as on normal days because there were only 4 days to go for Diwali. Many people celebrate the Diwali festival at home. It was a blissful day as we had a perfect sighting of the idol of Hanuman sitting in his mother's lap. With a mild pang of guilt, I asked the priest about the one who had invited me last time to consume the special prasad, but I had not been able to make it. When I saw him after he finished his duty, he told me that the priest I had met would have been assigned to another place.

A day later, on Hanuman Jayanti's birthday, I felt blessed as we were in the vicinity of the shrine again. This time, Janak and I went to the top floor, the highest place in Ayodhya. I could see the widened roads and the new set up of the shops all around. As we were coming down the exit at the back, I noticed a crew from a news channel. Subconsciously, I said, 'Ah, NDTV?' The reporter stopped and began to interview me. I was delighted when he referred to me as Dadaji, 'grandfather', and asked me about the developments around the town and my views on my recent visit. I felt elated.

We wandered down the new market, joining Bhakti Marg. It was bursting with pilgrims and locals who I thought looked equally spiritual. The shops were well stocked with pooja items, and there were souvenir shops all the way; some sweet meal shops looked irresistible. Dozens of pilgrims came from far and wide. It seemed most of them came for the first time, as they looked lost even in a small vicinity. I felt I had a nature's call, but it was hard to find a washroom. One under construction in the hotel, next to the shop where we bought some souvenirs, saved the embarrassment of using a secluded corner. Despite its size and new developments, Ayodhya retained the feel of a large village where you are likely to bump into the same crowd a few times, as most of the sites are literally next to each other. We had covered the length and breadth of the main sites of the town on foot. It gave me an opportunity to get a feel for the local atmosphere. But the strange thing was, I was keen to go out doing the same thing, walking again and again; it had such a magnetic pull.

KANAK BHAWAN

An impressive palace temple, Kanak Bhawan, is not far from the Rama Temple. Kaikeyi, Rama's stepmother, is supposed to have gifted the palace to Sita immediately after the marriage. It houses a temple on the far side, which was later renovated by King Vikramaditya and rebuilt again in 1891. It is one of the most elaborately detailed places in Ayodhya. A vast complex with a huge, marbled courtyard in the middle. The architecture looked marvellous. The echoes of an ancient past could be visualised in every direction. After ambling about the Bhawan, we joined some pilgrims sitting in the temple who were singing bhajans, evoking the emotions of devotional spirituality. They were singing the glory of Rama and clapping rhythmically to the sound of drumbeats. There were 3 pairs of idols of Rama and Sita of different sizes enshrined in the temple. I sat cross-legged on the floor mat, facing the deities for a few minutes.

As we were about to leave the place, an old man with a grey beard came up to us swiftly, as he was sitting on a pair of skates. He had his legs amputated. He began to describe the glory of the place. He looked very charming, skating around the courtyard. I captured his smiling face on my camera.

I wondered why Kaikeyi, who was a favourite queen of King Dashrath, should act so strangely. She had loved Rama and had even gifted the Kanak (Golden) Bhawan to his wife, Sita. Yet, on the night before Rama's coronation, she demanded that he be exiled for 14 years and her son Bharata be the King. Why would she be so cruel to Rama?

Fables have it that when the Gods realised that the coronation of Rama was not going to serve their purpose of banishing the terror of demons on Earth, they approached Saraswati, the Goddess of knowledge and wisdom, to obstruct the anointment of Rama as a King. Consequently, Saraswati possessed the mind and speech organ of Manthra, the hump-backed maidservant of Kaikeyi. In the palace, the queen was overjoyed to hear that her favourite Rama would be crowned as king the following day. But there was something else in store for Rama. Manthara made Kaikeyi believe that the coronation of Rama would leave her in an inferior position and that Bharata, her son, would be banished or killed. Manthara poisoned her mind successfully. Consequently, Kaikeyi asked the king, Dasharatha, for the 2 boons he had once offered her. Firstly, Rama should be banished to the forest for 14 years, and secondly, Bharata should be anointed as a king. It was only much later that Kaikeyi realised what she had done. She deeply repented her action.

It shows there must be a reason why sometimes an insignificant person like Manthara could change the life of an entire family.

MANI PARVAT

After visiting Kanak Bhawan, Babloo halted his vehicle in the car park of Mani Parvat, where only 3 cars indicated that it was not a popular site. It did not look like a Parbat, but a mound having an elevation of 65-70 feet tall certainly certified it as a hill.

A narrow zigzag dusty path was conspicuous beside a small wall and green bushes. It rose steadily, but the ascent was comfortable. Ubiquitous monkeys, some of them clutching young babies to their bellies, lined up around a felled tree. They were relishing the fruit thrown by the travellers. I was close enough to hear one of them nibbling on nuts. Another monkey with a little chap clinging to her on the ground near the tree root was flaring her nostrils while scratching her baby's back. I noticed a small monkey was following me and approaching fast; I swiftly threw the bag containing snacks towards him and quickened my pace as fast as I could!

It is believed that all kinds of gems and presents that Sita's father gave her at her wedding were stored up here. The pile of those gifts created a hill; therefore, it was called Money Parbat. There were various shrines atop the hill, but they did not look like temples from the outside.

Lord Buddha is believed to have preached the law of Dharma for 6 years from here. Guru Nanak Dev also stayed here for a while. There wasn't much to do on the top apart from viewing the sites in the town. We did not make eye contact with any monkey on the way down to our vehicle!

GUPTAR GHAT

If you do not visit this ghat, your journey will not be accomplished. Guptar ghat is the place where Lord Rama took Samadhi in the Saryu River. Apparently, most of the locals, too, gave up their lives along with the Lord. This area is a part of the army camp. We arrived here around 9.30 am. A few stalls selling fresh snacks like pakoras and roasted corn on the cob were apparent. There weren't many tourists, and the atmosphere on the ghats was calm and pleasant. We paid our obeisance in the various shrines.

As we came out of the Laxman temple, Janak and Indu noticed a small clay statue in light blue of Rama lying on the path near the cow's dung. It is supposed to be the same path that Rama walked towards the river. Indu pointed out the statue, which looked as if it had just been painted. I immediately picked it up respectfully. I wiped it with my clean hanky and kept looking at it for a good while. I thought about how somebody could drop it in such a way that it did not have any crack or scratch at all. I walked towards the river, knelt on the step, and washed the gracious statue before submerging it in the river Saryu. Although I had great feelings of excitement and nervousness at the same time, I had a lump in my throat while pushing it into the water. I took it as a divine blessing when the peacock-blue figure went down slowly in the clear waters.

Babloo insisted that we have a boat ride on the river. The views from the boat were unobstructed, and the sight of the temples looked appealing. It was a short ride but pleasant. It was an excellent place for an hour and a half's stroll on the peaceful and unspoilt ghat. Sitting on the benches along the ghat and watching the softly flowing river was blissful. But I was seized by a deep, unassailable sadness for a good while

MAKHAUDA DHAM

Makhauda Dham, also known as Manorama Tirtha, set the true stage for the beginning of the history of Lord Rama and the establishment of Rama Rajya. It is a revered pilgrimage site, situated around 15 kilometres north of Ayodhya.

The Putra-Kameshti (praying for sons) Yagna was performed here by sage Shringi after the advice of sage Vasistha. As the conclusion of the yajna drew near, a celestial being, representing Lord Brahma, arose from the sacrificial fire-pit and handed over a pot containing Kheer (Ladoo is mentioned in some places), saying that this must be consumed by the 3 wives of Dasharatha. Thus, the Princesses were conceived after the consumption. Since Kaushalya had consumed the largest portion, she gave birth to Rama. Kaikeyi gave birth to Bharata, and Sumitra gave birth to Lakshmana and Shatrughana.

As we entered Makhauda Dham through a well-decorated cement gate, it looked like an ordinary place from the outside. After meeting the main priest, we paid obeisance in a small ancient temple dedicated to Lord Shiva. Straight ahead towards the river was a vast Yagya place with a few sacrificial fire pits set up for many yagnas at a time; it was open from all sides. Some sadhus were busy with their daily chores. On the right, again, an open place under the tinned roof had a gathering of many young cadets or guides, where a man was delivering some sort of lecture. It was pleasant enough to spend some time, but we were running late to explore the next site.

DASHARATHA SAMADHI

As we reached there in the late evening, a young priest welcomed us. There wasn't a single pilgrim in sight as we were a bit late. It was so quiet that I could hear my own footsteps. It was a peaceful and fascinating site with unspoilt nature all around. I decided to visit the place at a later stage.

NANDIGRAM

The next morning, I stretched out of bed at 4.45 am and peeped through the curtain; it was jet-black. I rolled back into semi-slumber. When the alarm went off, I got into action mode immediately to avoid the crowd of pilgrims in Nandigram. I was excited to witness the place where Bharat spent 14 years waiting for his brother.

Nandigram is said to be the place where Bharat lived in a cave like a hermit and worshipped the Padukas of Rama. Bharat was an embodiment of virtue; he ruled the kingdom while Rama was in exile. He was so dedicated to his duties that he did not even enter Ayodhya. He preferred to be the servant of Lord Rama.

I watched nature go by from the tuk-tuk. In a way, I was enjoying the atmosphere and the cool early morning air. It felt like a world away from the chaotic roads of Ayodhya. Just before reaching Nandigram, a herd of cows was disturbed from their grazing by the roar of the tuk-tuk. They lifted their heads to stare; a couple of them kicked up dry dust from the muddy path. Perhaps they saw the noisy beast for the first time. It took over an hour to cover 20 kilometres.

The Bharat-Hanuman-Milan temple was tucked away behind the rows of tranquil tree lines, yet it was not hard to see from the road. As we passed the decorated cemented gate, the priest was coming out of the temple. He greeted us with a smile. As he began to show us around the complex before taking us to the main temple, I insisted that he give blessings of Lord Hanuman and Bharat before we went further. He obliged me with pleasure.

The deities of Bharat and Hanuman hugging each other in the shrine were so impressive that I stared at them for a good while. I prayed and admired the sculpture's creativity. The characters carved out of white marble looked full of life; it seemed as if they were about to speak. The depiction of the story was before my eyes. I could easily picture it.

This incident is well documented in the Rama Charit Manas. When Hanuman was carrying the mountain containing the Sanjeevani Booti (the life-saving plant from the Himalayas that would cure Lakshman's wounds incurred by the dreaded arrow of Indrajeet), he flew over the city of Ayodhya. He blocked the sun, turning a sunny day into night. Bharat looked up and noticed that an ape was flying with a massive mountain on his palm. He mistook his huge figure to be that of a demon and shot an arrow to bring him down. It hit Hanuman on his left knee, and as a result, he fell down, uttering 'Jai Sita-Ram'. Hearing the soothing name, Bharat immediately realised that he had made a mistake. When Bharat learnt the nature of Hanuman's errand, they embraced each other. Hanuman briefed Bharat about the entire incident. Bharat instructed Hanuman to reach Lanka before sunrise.

The priest gave the holy Charn Amrit after explaining the importance of the temple. We took advantage of being the only visitors at that time. The priest had more than enough time to show us around the entire complex.

The tiled narrow staircase on the left spiralled down to the basement that housed a few shrines. He began with the most elegant shrine of Bharat, where his statue was enshrined in a meditating posture. It was sculpted from a pure white marble monolith in such a way that when the lights were switched off, the mild shape of a crescent moon appeared on Bharat's head; then, he looked like Lord Shiva. And when the priest undid the curtains, he resembled Lord Vishnu. I cherished the mesmerising gem hidden in the basement.

Just opposite to this, there was a simple place where Lord Ram's Padukas, along with some rare Shaligrams in various sizes, were enshrined before Ram's photo.

In the small shrine on the left, there was an idol of Hanuman that represented the incident when he was hurt by an arrow shot by Bharat while he was carrying the mountain. Panditji showed us a special feature of Hanuman's idol. When he switched on the lights, Hanuman looked to be calm and calculative; when he switched off the lights, the idol appeared to be in a ferocious mood in the dark. It was fascinating.

It was time to explore the Bharat Gufa and 27 Teertha that were just next to this place. As I entered a huge complex, I saw a small Gufa where Bharat had stayed all those years. A small group of pilgrims was sitting on a mat listening to the priest. I bowed and listened to him for a couple of minutes and then went further to the right to see the main shrine in the complex. I could hear the couplets from the Rama Charit Manas before I entered the place. An idol of Bharat in a meditating posture and Ram's Padukas were housed in a small cave inside the temple. A photograph of Bharat hugging Hanuman was displayed on the side. The priest was busy worshipping while placing the incense sticks on the stand. It is believed to be the place where Hanuman came to convey the message of Ram's victory.

Rama had summoned Hanuman to go to Nandigram and inform Bharat about his arrival, as Rama knew that if he did not reach there by the last day of the 14th year of exile, Bharat would give up his life. As predicted, Bharat lit up the pyre and performed paridakshana (circumambulation) before jumping into it. Hanuman saw him from the sky and uttered the glory of Rama. He recognised Hanuman and hugged him tightly. Hanuman told Bharat the news he was waiting for. For a moment, my mind took me back to The Ramayana era.

Rama did not go straight to Ayodhya after eliminating Ravana. Firstly, he consecrated the Shiv-lingam in Rameshwaram, then stopped at Sage Bhardwaj's Ashram in Prayagraj to pay respect, and then went to Chitrakoot to thank other rishis for their advice. Before meeting Bharat, Rama Chander visited Shringverpur to thank Guha for his help. It is believed that Sita also thanked the River Ganga for reducing its flow and becoming shallow and calmer when they crossed it.

When I strolled towards another significant site, an old man greeted me with a smile. It was a place where Bharat used to meditate under an old Banyan tree. It was peculiar to see that most of its roots were not touching or going underground but growing upwards onto the tree.

He pointed at the top and said, "The tree is so dense that the rays of the sun do not reach the ground."

He looked excited to show me around. I followed him to a special place where the 'Well' known as '27 Teertha' was situated. It was covered with some removable wooden planks to protect it from dust and dry leaves. It contained the water from 27 holy rivers. The holy water was believed to be collected for the ceremony at the time of Lord Ram's coronation.

The old man removed a long piece of wood and asked me if I wanted to wash my face for good luck. The temperature was already on its way to 30 degrees. I got greedier and took off my T-shirt and trousers in a flash. I sat down on a cemented platform in shorts and asked him to pour some water on my head. He pulled out the brass bucket that was tied with a rope, fetched the water from the well, and splashed it on my head. He rushed to get some more water a few more times. It felt so pleasant that I did not stop him from blessing me with cool, holy water. I did not have any towels to dry myself. He offered me his thin red scarf that he was wearing around his neck. I accepted it gladly. He was sweat-soaked, breath gasping, but full of enthusiasm to explain the history. It was a pleasure to listen to someone who was knowledgeable and dedicated to his work. There were some more pilgrims around who asked him to provide some water to wash their faces. I offered my help, but he refused. A well-deserved remuneration brought a big smile to his face.

It took only a few minutes to reach the equally, if not more important, place where Rama met Bharat for the first time after his exile. This Bharat-Rama Milap temple was small, but the pond where Bharat used to bathe every day was spread over a vast area. My heart sank a little when I saw that this significant complex was neglected compared to Ayodhya. It is believed that it was the place where Rama, Lakshman and Bharat shaved off their jetted hair and wore royal costumes. As the entire royal family was present to receive them, Queen Kashayla adorned Sita with the best ornaments and attire before proceeding to Ayodhya. It was as if I had drifted back to that era when the priest manning the shrine was explaining the history.

It was the new moon night of the Hindu Lunisolar month of Kartik - the Amavasya night - when they all, along with Hanuman and others, returned to Ayodhya for the first time after conquering Lanka. The streets and houses all the way from Nandigram to Ayodhya were decorated with lights and buntings. The entire city of Ayodhya was adorned with flowers and streamers and was illuminated with countless clay lamps to welcome the victorious Rama. All the subjects welcomed them, reciting hail to Rama. There was happiness all around the kingdom. Sweets and gifts were distributed to everyone. Many fireworks snaked up into the sky above Ayodhya; many a time, the sky looked full of colourful sparking stars. The colossal crowds in convivial spirits, feasting on various sweets and food items and fireworks all day, underlined the significance of true happiness. That is how the festival of 'Diwali' originated. It is still the most celebrated festival to date. In fact, it is celebrated all over the world now and is referred to as 'the Indian Christmas'. Diwali may be a metaphorical triumph of light over darkness and good over evil, but for Hindus, it is a religious festival. Isn't it ironic that Nandigram is comparatively ignored in the celebrations, even though, according to Rama Charit Manas, it was Nandigram and not Ayodhya that first received Lord Rama when he returned from exile?

SARYU RIVER AND GHATS

The busy itinerary of the day was exhausting, but I still enjoyed it intensely. Ayodhya is a place of faith for the thronging pilgrims, where the morning starts with the ringing of bells and mantras and the evening with aarti and the fragrance of incense sticks. It was a beautiful sight to see the ghats illuminated with earthen lamps flickering all around; lights twinkled on the distant ghats. Some pilgrims were still enjoying a dip in the Saryu waters as they believed they came here for purification and to wash away their sins. I lowered myself into the water on the Ghat but immediately jumped out; it was a bit too cold for me!

I witnessed the enthusiasm of the devotees at evening aarti; some of them were clapping and chanting as loudly as they could. The sound of drumbeats and the blowing of conch shells invigorated the atmosphere. Babloo made a request to the priest, and he handed over the brass aarti pot to me for a few seconds; I prayed and swayed in full vigour. It was a moment of heavenly feelings that gave me spiritual uplifting. No matter how many times you may have seen the aarti on television or in films, nothing prepares you for being present there in the evening. Coming to Ayodhya and not witnessing aarti is like going to Paris and missing the Eiffel Tower.

NAGESHWARA TEMPLE

Janak and I could have walked to the Nageshwara temple as it was just beside the Rama ki Paidi, but Babloo insisted that I should go in his vehicle. I was keen to pay my obeisance at the oldest temple of Ayodhya.

The Nageshwar Nath, another name for Shiva, was built by Kush, a son of Rama. According to the mythical tale, King Kush lost his amulet while bathing in the river Saryu. A Nag-Kanya – a serpent damsel – retrieved it from the base of the river and returned it to the king. She instantly fell in love with him. As she was a devotee of Shiva, Kush erected this temple for her. It is believed that this is the only temple that survived when Ayodhya was abandoned until the reign of Chandragupta Vikramaditya. The entire city became desolate after Rama's ascent to his heavenly abode. It is also claimed that by means of this temple, Vikramaditya was able to locate Ayodhya and other shrines in the city around 50 BCE.

Apart from being a place of historical and religious significance, I could feel the holiness and divine presence in the air. I could hear the praise of Lord Shiva some distance from the shrine. The simple exterior of the temple was unpromising, but when I glanced inside the place, it was fascinating. It was full of young men who were bathing the Shiva Lingam with milk while reciting his praise in loud, rhythmic voices. Some of them were washing walls and the floor amongst the thick smoke of incense sticks. The atmosphere was one of happiness and celebration.

When we visited the place for Diwali celebrations in November 2023, it was decorated with lights and flowers all around the temple. We arrived at the right time when the evening aarti was about to begin, creating a complete spiritual atmosphere.

DIWALI ON RAMA KI PAIDI

We were in Ayodhya 4 days prior to Diwali in 2023 to enjoy the atmosphere, witnessing the new Rama Temple under construction before its consecration on the 22nd of January 2024 by the Prime Minister, Mr Narendra Modi. I was expecting a flood of people in the town, but there was the usual crowd of pilgrims and tourists; this may be due to the fact that most Hindus celebrate the festival of Diwali at home.

Most of Ayodhya's tourist attractions, from temples to ghats and roadside lighting to shops, were beautifully decorated with colourful lights and streamers all around. This was complemented by the artful display of lights by every household. The markets and bazaars selling sweet cakes, contemporary designs of earthen lamps, gift items, and eateries were packed with tourists and locals buying their essentials for the festival. Despite the substantial developments and improvements in infrastructure, the city not only retained its cultural identity but also enhanced its character and charm. It was a privilege to spend a few days in Ayodhya.

Rama ki Paidi, also known as the Swarg Dwar (gateway to heaven), was the prime place to enjoy during the Diwali festival. It was situated near Naya ghat. It was a beautiful site where a water channel was connected to the river Saryu. The whole length of the water channel was lined with red sandstone tiles. The flight of steps that went towards the river looked fabulous. The water in the Paidi is drawn from the Saryu River by motor pumps. That was the place where 21 lakh earthen pots were lit on Chhoti Diwali. The scenery at night was rapturous.

It seemed Ayodhya was on its way to get its pride and glory back to its heyday. Ayodhya once considered a small town, looked to be evolving into a globally acclaimed holy and tourist city with world-class infrastructure such as an international airport, a newly built railway station, highways, and top-class accommodation. The outlook of markets, Bhakti Marg, Rama Path, etc., was drenched in The Ramayana era. I thought it was impossible to get lost, but I did, though, for a little while.

The day before Diwali, known as Chhoti Diwali, is celebrated with pomp and is shown in Ayodhya. On that morning, I asked Babloo to take me to the place where I could donate some money. There was only one official place near the main gate that accepted cash/cards. I did not know until Babloo mentioned it that it was the same office where they issued free passes to witness the live aarti every day at the Rama

Temple. When we requested passes, the gentleman told us to wait for a while. My eyes lit up. After a few minutes, he asked me to come inside the office. He was very polite and helpful. He issued me the required computerised passes and advised me to be there on time as necessary security checks were conducted before entry. Unquestionably, it was a very satisfying and memorable moment. There were still a few hours to go, but my mind was imagining so many things. I could not get my head around the fact that we got the entry passes to witness the ceremony of the evening aarti. I felt very fortunate to participate in such a spiritual atmosphere.

As we entered, it appeared to be an abode of Lord Rama indeed. It was a visual feast to see the new Rama Temple being built on the right. The view of the deity looked fabulous. The first floor of the shrine looked nearly complete. I bowed the moment I saw the temple.

Everything conspired to be perfect for the evening. There were only 35-40 seats in front of the shrine behind the steel barricading. We were sitting in the idyllic spot, right opposite the deities. I had rarely felt so cosy as well as content before. The view of the idol of infant Rama was majestic. It was fascinating to see the idols so close to us. The view of the infant Rama was majestic, and the atmosphere was thrilling.

When the bells began to peel and the priest started to chant mantras before aarti, I was glowing with excitement and festive cheerfulness. I was asked to keep silent, but my excitement got the better of me; it was impossible not to feel a surge of it. This was a magical moment, like something from a distant dream. One day, the Lord you have been worshipping all your life is before your eyes. And that day is also the eve of Diwali.

I was literally broken down in tears, bewildered by a mixture of excitement, pride, and contentment. Hand on heart, I have to say, I never imagined that I would be a part of this special occasion. For me, it was also a gesture to honour and give thanks. I had no desire to leave the site for even a second, but I had to follow the rules. As I was coming out, my mind decelerated; even my heartbeat seemed to slow down, and a sense of calm took over.

It seemed the entire Ayodhya was in a celebratory mood on the night before Diwali. Twenty-one thousand oil-filled earthen pots were lit in Rama ki Paidi and its vicinity; it was a sight to relish. The place was so noisy with selfie-takers that there was no room to move freely; even then, the actual feel of the atmosphere was very much there. Many a time, I tried to walk around like a travel writer, but within a few minutes, the spirituality took over.

As we turned around from Lata Mangeshkar, the hum of street food vendors offering piping hot snacks made me stop at a stall that was frying double-bread pakora. I thought a light snack should be justified. A large crowd was waiting for their turn. It was worth the wait; it was so tasty that sheer greediness made me order another plate despite being full!

It was the contrast offered by the magnificent sights of Rama ki Paidi and the spiritual ambience that delighted me most. The collision of hum in the temples and the spectacular viewing of the laser-guided show depicting The Ramayana story. The heavenly and earthly atmospheres were equally enjoyable.

Every time I left Ayodhya, I felt a sinking feeling in my stomach. On the last day of my trip, I retired to my bed with great relief, but sleep was miles away. I had mixed feelings. I felt sad that the trip to Ayodhya had ended but content that the journey had turned out to be the way I had envisaged.

SHRINGVERPUR

Before setting off to Chitrakoot from Pryagraj, I decided to detour to Shringverpur in Kaushambi district. It is widely believed that the city got its name from the sage Shringi. It was the capital city of the Nishadraj Kingdom. The king, Guha, reigned over this place as per Valmiki Ramayana. We visited Sage Bhardwaj's Ashram too. Janak and Indu were talking about the aarti ceremony at the Sangam ghat in Pryagraj on the previous night, where the moment was made more special when the priest handed over the aarti pot to conduct it along with him. It took just an hour to cover 40 kilometres; the road became quieter and more isolated as we came out of the city. It was situated on the banks of the holy River Ganga.

Shringverpur is an important site for Hindus, as 3 significant incidents took place here. First and foremost, when Rama stayed here for a night before proceeding to Prayagraj on his exile for a period of 14 years. Then Bharat passed through it when he was on his way to Chitrakoot to request Rama to return to Ayodhya. It is believed that when Guha showed the place where Rama rested and spent the night, Bharat fell on the ground and cried consistently, blaming himself for Rama's fate. The last event was when Rama and Sita came here to thank Guha and the River Ganga after killing Ravana before going back to Ayodhya. The river had become shallow and calm while they were crossing it in Kevat's boat.

The entrance to the place was impressive, and the large statues of Rama, Sita, and Lakshman sitting on chariots were enshrined. Nearby, a large statue of Hanuman in a small temple was enshrined. The riverbank was beautifully arranged with long benches and set up by the pundits to perform their daily religious rituals and other activities. A few pilgrims, after the dip, were changing into dry outfits that they brought with them. Many devotees were ascending a comfortable flight of a few steps to the temple of Shanta Devi, the wife of sage Shringi. It was a serene place. Before we could drive away, a man selling a few kinds of fruits on his four-wheel cart stopped and asked us to buy his product. He looked so innocent that I bought 2 kilograms of ripe mangoes. The mango was so succulent that I barely noticed the juice that ran down my chin and then onto my shirt; I told him to keep the change.

We went to the Samadhi of sage Shringi and then to Rama Chaura that was close to it. This place is famous for the fact that Rama stayed here under the tree for a night and asked his subjects to return to Ayodhya. This was their first night of exile. Also, Rama, Sita, and Lakshman denounced their royal robes and changed their attire to that worn by ascetics here.

Guha met Rama and paid homage to him. He was a childhood friend of Rama. Whenever Rama went hunting in that area, Guha also accompanied him and used to arrange refreshments and a place to rest. This time, Guha felt extremely sad to see them spending the night on an uncomfortable bed of Kusha, the grass strands, under a Banyan tree. He asked Rama to stay comfortably with him at his place for a night.

Rama embraced Guha and said, "I cannot accept your hospitality as I am under a vow not to enter a town."

The next morning, at the bank of the Ganga, Rama asked Kevat, a boatman, to take them across the river.

Kevat said to Lord Rama, "I have heard that by a mere touch of your foot, a stone had turned into a woman. I fear what would happen to my old boat with the touch of your feet. But if you insist, please let me wash your feet before entering the boat."

Recognising the love of Kevat, Rama kept quiet. Nishadraj and Guha visited the place to resolve the issue. Rama submitted to the love and affection of his devotee and allowed Kevat to wash his feet with the water of Ganga and drink it to show his reverence towards his Lord. Guha asked for permission from Rama to go along with them. Rama agreed. They all went to Pryagraj to seek blessings from the sage, Bhardwaj. The sage not only blessed them but also sent 4 people to help them cross the river, Jamuna. Upon reaching Chitrakoot, Rama asked Guha to return to serve his kingdom, which he did reluctantly.

Then, we moved to the prime site of Ramchura. The place where Kevat washed Ram's feet has been marked by a small platform. It was named Ramchura to commemorate the incident. There were many other small temples around the place. The place itself was very serene, yet looked neglected. I could not stay longer as the clock was ticking fast.

CHITRAKOOT

Early in the morning, after visiting Shringverpur, we set off for the eagerly awaited sector of Chitrakoot and its surrounding areas that are blessed by the Gods and sanctified by the faith of their devotees. Right from the start, my mind was busy imagining the dense jungle where Rama, Sita, and Lakshmana wandered for more than 11 years. Janak, Ashok, and Indu, in the back of the car, slipped comfortably into slumber mode. By the time I was trying to visualise the forest where Rama was advised by the sage Bharadwaj to stay, the periphery of the Northern Vindhya range of lush mountains was before my eyes. It took more than 4 hours in November 2012, but this time in 2023, it was a smooth journey of just 2 and a half hours.

Chitrakoot literally means a beautiful mountain. It is a symbol of faith and a holy hotspot for devotees. It bears the pride of its heritage humbly, like a prominent sage unimpressed by his own religious acumen. Chitrakoot is a place of deep mythological relevance steeped in ancient history, where calm and repose pervade even now. It is the sort of place where every stone you look upon dislodges history, and every blade of grass you touch has a story to tell. It is one of those towns that could be measured by simply walking around. Tulsidas is believed to have visited the place to meditate and seek divine inspiration when he was about to begin the magnum opus on Rama's life, Ramcharitmanas. At one time, Chitrakoot was under the Chandela dynasty, and later, it was ruled by the Marathas. The British took over control in 1802 and governed there until 1947.

As we entered the Chitrakoot area, the ubiquitous greenery unfolded before us. The auto-rickshaw drivers were waiting for the incoming visitors along the roadside. Chitrakoot has not made so much as a blip on the tourist radar, yet all Hindus know its significance. Since the Bharatiya Janata Party won the elections in 2014, the signs of development in this region of Bundelkhand could be seen all around, including the basic infrastructure, roads, hotel accommodations, and other facilities for visitors.

RAMA GHAT

Chitrakoot's spiritual legacy stretches back to ancient times. It was in these dense forests that Rama spent most of his time during the exile. Many sages and poets have sought solace through its tranquil nature. They have drawn inspiration and spiritual strength from its serene beauty. Some people say you can travel right through Chitrakoot and its major sites in one day as they are next to each other. That can only be done if you have no soul and heart but just ticking off your bucket list. Subconsciously, I had underestimated the scenic beauty and the number of sites to explore. I allocated 2 days, but a few hours into my trip, I promised myself to come back as soon as possible. When I came back in 2023, it was just a stopover for a night.

Chitrakoot has so much to see, and you cannot help but dither slightly over which site to explore first. After a brief rest, we decided to cherish the evening aarti. In fact, I relaxed a bit too long. As we reached the ghat, the aarti ceremony was just accomplished. The Rama Ghat showed a deep and abiding faith in the rituals that honour the sanctity of Chitrakoot; the devotees were still wandering about. I felt as if I was bereft of the blessings of River Mandakini. Suddenly, I noticed some flames in the brass pot, which they had used for aarti rituals, were still alive and glowing with full vigour. Fortunately, the head priest - Panditji - who conducted the ceremony, came over and gave me the blessings. Panditji explained to me the importance of the famous Mathagajendreshwara temple, overlooking the river; it was dedicated to Lord Shiva. The priest began to walk toward the shrine and asked me to follow him. I quickly went back and told Janak to wait for me until I returned.

The temple was located on a small hill with easily walkable steps. It is believed that Rama prayed here and asked Raja – God's – permission to live in the area. As I entered a small sanctum, the chanting of mantras in loud voices was in full swing. There were many priests who were so engrossed in chanting the mantras that their faces were red, and sweat was running down their foreheads. It was an extremely traditional way of praying. As they finished the ceremony, the head priest, who was the first one to bow before the base of the Shiva Lingam, picked up some rose petals and ate them as prasad. He asked me to do the same. I felt privileged and fortunate to witness such a spiritual moment. It felt as if Lord Shiva came down and showered some blessings. Panditji gave me his visiting card and advised me to pay obeisance at Bharata temple, where he believed Rama had stayed for 5 days to persuade him to go back to Ayodhya.

Most of Chitrakoot's religious and leisure activities are in the very central Rama Ghat. The importance of the place is so great that the town of Chitrakoot has almost become synonymous with Rama Ghat. A dozen small boats piled from the ghat. Some of them were sublimely luxurious, some distinctly decorated with streamers and flowers; the colourful lights on all of them attracted everyone's attention. I was overwhelmed watching the boats moving anticlockwise in a loop. As we visited a small temple of Bharata, the Charan-paduka representing Lord Rama in front of the deities was the highlight of the shrine. The priest put them on our heads as blessings. We followed the same route to visit the Lakshmana temple.

The next morning, I started my day at 5 am. After visiting Hanuman Dhara, Janak and I were keen to have a boat ride that we could not take the night before. It seemed Rama Ghat swirled to life even before dawn. With the very first ray of the sun that gleams upon the river, Rama Ghat stirs into life as the pilgrims take a purifying dip in the waters and invoke the blessing of the Lord. It is believed that Rama, Sita, and Lakshmana had a dip on their arrival and during their exile.

As we were strolling, a young boy came up to sell some offerings for the holy river. I went down the steps, washed my face, and slowly pushed the paper boat of flowers into the slow-moving water. Janak did not take an extra outfit; therefore, she had to be content with the same process rather than having a dip. We took a ride in the rippling waters. The views of the banks of the river were impressive. Rama's new temple, which is white on the right, was eye-catching. Some sadhus, surrounded by devotees, seemed to indicate a festival. As we went further, a tall statue of Hanumana was right upon us; it looked fabulous. The entire atmosphere was suffused with the chanting of Vedic hymns and mantras through the melodious tunes.

There was a place with Tulsi Das's statue near Bharata Ghat, where Tulsi Das is believed to have seen Rama when he was preparing some sandalwood paste to apply on his forehead. Fable has it that Rama, as a child, appeared before Tulsi. Rama had asked him to apply tilak, the paste, on his forehead, which he did without recognising the Lord. At this juncture, Hanumana helped Tulsi recognise Rama by appearing in the disguise of a parrot and murmuring the verse in his ear.

He said, "Chitrakoot ke ghat pe, paee santan ki bheer. Tulsi Das Chandan ghise, tilak det Raghuveer." It meant Tulsi Das applied sandalwood paste on Ram's forehead at the crowded Ghat of Chitrakoot.

We sat on the steps near Bharata Ghat for a while and watched the moonbeams dancing on the rippling surface of the river. It felt like the sound of ripples was Rama telling the story of his journey. It was hard not to be caught up in devout enthusiasm.

HANUMAN DHARA

It was still dark when Janak and I left the hotel to visit Hanuman Temple on a mountain. We bought the offerings from the only shop that was open at the time. The shop lady warned us about the mischievous monkeys and advised us to climb up steadily to avoid getting breathless. The thrill of climbing up 600-plus steps was more satisfying than worrying about the monkeys snatching the bag of offerings. After a comfortable start, the steps eased into a gentle ascent. It took 40 minutes to reach the shrine. The scenery was quite pleasing. The higher we went, the better it got. I could clearly spot the winding path where some devotees were climbing in small groups. I had uninterrupted views of green fields stretching out in the distance.

The temple on the edge of the hill enshrines a rare idol of Hanuman where a continuous spring of water falls on the chest of the deity. It is believed that the cascade was created by Rama to ease the hardship and pain after he set fire to the city of Lanka. Lord Rama is believed to have suggested to Hanuman that he stay on this mountain. He shot an arrow to create a narrow stream of water to relieve Hanuman's pain.

We were the second to reach the temple; the first one was a solitary man from Bhopal who wanted to get the Lord's blessings before leaving. The first sight of Hanuman brought a sudden upsurge of energy, and the tiredness of the strenuous climb evaporated immediately. The curls of fragrant smoke of incense sticks drifted through the verandah. The head priest was delighted to see us and explained the relevant history of the place. He cheerfully gave us the blessings and prasad of ash in a small packet, which I still have in my possession.

A streak of water gushing out from the hillock fell into a concrete tank after touching the deity. It was situated just below the shrine next to the steps on the left. The water that is filtered down is not only considered holy but also useful in terms of irrigation. We took our time wandering around before heading for Sita Rasoi – the Kitchen. It took another 55-60 steps to reach the place. There was a small temple dedicated to Sita Mata, which was manned by a grey-haired man. Next door, on the right, there was a verandah where Sita Mata used to prepare food for 7 sages; the statues of all of them near the back wall looked attractive.

We enjoyed the serenity of the mountain during daybreak, with only the sound of birds chirping. The descent was quite comfortable. I noticed many pilgrims wore hand-knitted caps and mufflers to protect themselves from the early morning frost, but I was sure that after ascending a few steps, they would put them back in their bags.

Our trip in 2023 to the place did not take as long as the service of the cable car to the temple was easy and comfortable.

KAMADGIRI MOUNTAIN

After a heavy breakfast of potato-stuffed parathas, I was ready to explore the most illustrious mountain of superb fairy-tale significance, the Kamadgiri. Chitrakoot makes the most of Kamadgiri Mountain as it is believed to have been the abode of Rama, Sita, and Lakshmana during their exile. It is a charismatic mountain of spiritual importance and is geared up to eulogise the charm of Rama in its surroundings. The Sanskrit word Kamadgiri means the mountain that fulfils all wishes and desires. Coincidentally, it appears like a bow from the aerial view.

The temple of Lord Kamta Nath, the principal deity, is enshrined with only his face visible. The entire mountain is supposed to be the rest of the body. The main temple is situated at the front of the hill, where the middle area is devoted to Lord Rama. It is flanked by the idols of Sita and Lakshmana. Before settling down, Rama worshipped Kamta Nath and asked for his permission to stay over there.

Kamadgiri constitutes one of the parikrama paths. Pilgrims strongly believe that circumambulating the mountain will fetch them many of the boons that they desire. The pilgrimage paths around the mountain are about 5 kilometres. It was built by Partap Kunwari, the queen of Bundela King Maharaja Chhatra Sal, in 1725. The forested hill is skirted all along the base by a chain of temples and is venerated even today as the holy embodiment of Rama. The serenity of the hilly terrain is attributed to the deep woods.

Our driver dropped us near the Kamta Nath shrine, where streams of pilgrims from other provinces were gathered. Ashok and Indu did not want to negotiate 5 kilometres on foot; therefore, we hired 2 rickshaws, the only option available at the time. The rickshaw pullers were going faster than we wanted. The path of the entire loop was smooth enough, yet a few ascents and descents at bends gave us scary moments. A young boy voluntarily pushed both vehicles to turn by turn. It was great fun, but I asked them to go slow. Occasionally, there were apprehensive, childlike giggles at places.

Soon, we were at the gate of the Bharata Milap complex, where a few mischievous monkeys greeted us by snatching a bag of snacks. As we entered, the place looked fabulous, with a few yellow chhatris on the right and a small temple straight ahead depicting Bharata taking Padukas from Rama. This was the place where Bharata met Rama to convince him to return to Ayodhya. There were many pilgrims around the hexagon chhatris where the imprints of Rama's, Bharata's, and other members of the family displayed the incident. The calmness and the crowd were soothing at the same time. The holiness of the place was retained remarkably; it gave me a pilgrimage feel. I was glad that I witnessed the site as it was only accessible by way of parikrama of the mountain.

At this point, I realised that we should have come on foot like others to enjoy the atmosphere all around. We passed several small shrines along the way. It is believed that the mountain from the inside is somewhat hollow, with an underground network of caves where some sages meditated. But I could not figure out anything like this at any stage. As we were weaving back to accomplish our journey, the rickshaw-puller pointed at the hill and explained that the hill was called Lakshmana Parbat where he stayed and kept vigil for Rama and Sita at night. I decided to leave it for the next trip. The ride was hilarious and joyous. It was arguably the most rewarding and extraordinary place in the area.

SATI ANUSUYA TEMPLE

It took 45 minutes to cover 16 kilometres to Sati Anusuya's place. It has rightly been cited as one of the most revered places in Chitrakoot. It was the kind of region where you could be nervous about missing the right exit on the main road; you could easily wander alone. The scenic journey through the green woods glued me to the car window. I could visualise how and why the prominent sages preferred to meditate in these forests. The endless greenery on both sides of the road cast the shadow of good sites ahead.

The temple of Sati Anusuya is dedicated to a woman as its name suggests. Anusuya means free from jealousy and envy. Literally speaking, she was an exemplary woman known for her loyalty, fidelity, and devotion. Anusuya was the wife of a great sage, Atri, who was the eldest of the 7 sages created by Lord Brahma during the process of the creation of the Universe.

Valmiki related that at one time there was no rain in the Chitrakoot area for over a decade. There was a severe famine, and nothing was left to eat or drink, even for animals and birds. Anusuya performed some intense austerities and consequently brought down the River

Mandakini to Earth. This led to the greenery and the forests growing, and consequently, it removed the suffering of all sages and the animals.

Rama and Sita visited the place during their exile. Mata Anusuya narrated the stories of the duties of a woman and gave a discourse on piety and its importance. This area was the dense forest of Dandakaranya where Ravana had appointed Khar and Viradha as its rulers. The place was infected by the terror of demons. The sages asked Rama to eliminate the rakshasas so that they could meditate in peace.

The temple of Sati Anusuya was tucked away on a hillside on the bank of the River Mandakini. I was enjoying the atmosphere of stillness when some boisterous monkeys began to chase each other on the branches of the trees. They were howling and growling; it was quite a roar. We kept away from them. I noticed a big fat monkey was staring at me, unblinking and intensively. He began to come towards us lethargically. I asked Janak to ignore him and keep the bag of snacks tucked under her arm. He inspected us and strolled casually towards his mates while scratching his backside. As we went further near the temple, I could hear the calls of peacocks in the distance. It was also soothing to hear the chirping of plenty of birds. I could smell the scents of the green forest and feel the cool air wafting through the trees.

The place is blessed with lush green trees along with a calm river, yet nobody seemed to be enjoying the atmosphere. A group of 3 women and a few children were tossing some pieces of bread into the water where a frenzy of fish was surfacing, picking up the crumbs and disappearing. I enjoyed watching them too. All the pilgrims were rushing to go into a vast temple where, at the entrance, a massive colourful wheel and statues looked fabulous.

There was pin-drop silence in the entire area of the temple; the peace and tranquillity were occasionally broken by some pilgrims asking priests about the history. There were many Hindu scriptures and murals all around. Some small shrines explaining the story of Sati and Rama's journey were more crowded. The ashram in the vicinity housed the statues of Sati Anusuya, Sage Atri, Dattatreya, and Durvasa, which looked attractive. It was a great hidden treasure where history was spoken through the depiction of scenes of various incidents.

After a few hours of intense touring, my body felt that it had had enough of a workout, therefore I needed some carbohydrates before collapsing into bed for a few hours.

GUPT GODAVARI

We reached the vicinity of Gupt Godavari in a few minutes from the hotel. Nestled at the base of a majestic hillock, Gupt Godavari is a network of 2 caves accessible by a narrow opening. Each cave had a shrine and a natural spring from which water seeped out. I am not a person who enjoys going inside caves or any other claustrophobic sites. Some pilgrims told me that inside the caves, it was reasonably comfortable to move around. The atmosphere was quite conducive to exploration.

As I entered the first cave, it looked dark and damp. A couple of drops of water fell on my head from the ceiling. The claustrophobic air of the cave hung around my head like a steel helmet. 'Hail to Ram,' a voice out of my mouth eerily prompted, and as the collective voices in return resounded 'Jai Shri Ram,' I gained a lot of confidence. As my eyes adjusted to the darkness, I could figure out the beauty of the place. There was more fluorescent light further ahead. This cave was like a small tank which was perpetually fed by a small stream of water; it was not very deep. This tank is known as Sita Kund. I looked around carefully and waded through the gently flowing water.

I did not have any claustrophobic feeling upon entering the second cave. The water in this cave was nearly touching my knees. I just rolled up my trousers and walked gingerly through the water to the far side. It was somewhat intimidating as some pilgrims were rushing and splashing. I took my time as I did not want to tumble in the middle of the cave. The small pebbles on the floor helped me to have smooth manoeuvrings.

The water in the cave is supposed to be the river Godavari, emerging as a perennial stream from the rocks deep inside the cave and then flowing down to the stream where Sita used to bathe. This stream that flowed through the caves gave this place the name 'Gupt -hidden - Godavari'.

There were 2 indentations that looked like thrones. Rama used to sit there and hold court in the caves. A massive rock hanging from the ceiling looked strange. It is believed that those were the remains of the demon Mayank. It was the place where Rama encountered his first fight with a demon in Chitrakoot. The fables have it that the demon had the audacity to steal Sita's attire, which had been given by Sati Anusuya. Rama killed the demon and hung him upside down in the cave.

There were 2 tanks outside where the water was gushing out from the caves, and then it disappeared suddenly, creating an aura of mystery. A cluster of very old trees on the right was worshipped by some pilgrims. The roasting of fresh sweet corn on the cob was a common sight in the area. It prompted me to find a perfect excuse at a perfect place for another recess and a break before heading towards Sphatik Shila in the tranquil forest. As usual, I became greedy again to have another serving while enjoying the natural atmosphere.

SPHATIK SHILA

Sphatik Shila – stone – is a place marked by 2 flat boulders. It is believed to be the place where Rama and Sita often feasted their eyes on the serene surroundings of Chitrakoot. This place of natural beauty had every shade of green all around, with the River Mandakini flowing calmly nearby.

We walked to a gigantic rock on the riverbank. The Sphatik Shila is worshipped as it bears the footprints of Rama and Sita. It was their usual place for romantic evenings, and Rama used to adorn Sita with a necklace of flowers. We took 2 parikramas, as suggested by the priest, one for Rama and another for Sita. There were more monkeys than pilgrims in the vicinity. Janak has always been mad about feeding them. She bought 3 bags full of nuts and seeds, but they lasted only one minute. Ironically, there were many sacks full of nuts and seeds, but the monkeys never went for them, even though the vendors did not seem to chase them away.

On every trip to Chitrakoot, I felt that I had an overwhelming experience. I needed plenty of time to absorb and explore the natural beauty and the atmosphere thoroughly.

TULSI MANDIR IN RAJAPUR

It is almost going without saying that India has rare temples with a unique history. I had never known that the birthplace of Goswami Tulsi Das in Rajapur was so near before I arrived at Chitrakoot. Apparently, there is a temple known as Shri Tulsi Janam Kutir which is dedicated to him. It is situated on the banks of the River Yamuna in Nidhi Gram in the District of Banda.

It took an hour and a half to cover 40 km from Chitrakoot on the narrow and dusty road through the busy market of Rajapur. When we reached the town, it looked as if the green market, grain market, poultry market, and every other kind of shop were trading on the same road. It took another half an hour to cover 500 metres before we could find the street leading to the temple; it was choked with morning shoppers inspecting local produce spread out on the road. It took more than 15 minutes to cover the frenetic 100 metres, fending off hawkers on both sides, weaving between cows, and dodging two-wheelers.

The street that led to Tulsi Kutir was clean but narrow; only one car could pass at a time. With a hoot and honk, we came to a halt in the small car park. The noise of sounding horns and vendors shouting for their products totally drifted away. But still, it did not look like a touristy place. Even my taxi driver, who plied his trade regularly on the Prayagraj to Chitrakoot route, did not know anything about this place. It was a congested place that deserved better access.

When I came out of the taxi, my frustration evaporated with the cool breeze and the sight of the beautiful scenery. The view of the shimmering flowing water of the Yamuna at the base of the hill and the dwellings on the opposite side was eye-soothing. I gazed all around while doing some stretching exercises. The symmetrical pink-stone steps leading to the ghats looked striking at first glance. They were clean and wide but very steep.

The temple complex does not have a fabulous look from the outside, but inside, it is a treasure of unmatched history. It is home to some of the unique scriptures. An ancient temple of Tulsi Das is situated on the edge of a hill. It is tucked away behind the populous community. Its sprawling vicinity and a steel bridge on the Yamuna River looked serene in the backdrop. The village across the river was supposed to be the place where Tulsi's in-laws lived. The entire area looked not only beautiful but had great importance in the context of The Ramayana, and yet it was barely visited by pilgrims.

The Tulsi Kuteer does not look like a temple from the outside. After entering an ordinary-looking small structure, I saw one Panditji reciting some Chapais (verses) of The Ramayana in a soft voice on the left and on the right, the book of Ramayana was opened on a reading stand, but Panditji was missing from his seat. The main shrine was manned by another priest with a long greyish beard. He was busy with the female devotee who was presenting some offerings to the deities of Lord Rama, Sita, and Lakshmana. I, too, looked at them respectfully and then bowed. They were beautifully adorned with sequinned yellow satin outfits. On the left, a beautiful idol of Hanuman was enshrined, and on the right, there was another small temple behind the glass door where an elegant statue of Hanuman was incorporated into the platform.

I moved in front of the main deities and began to take photographs. As I clicked my camera on the main shrine where Panditji was giving some offerings back to the lady, in a flash, he used his free hand to draw the curtain in front of the deities. Obviously, he was irritated and pulled the curtain to stop me from taking any more photographs. I did not realise that he would react like this, but I complied with his order happily.

Before I could apologise, he shouted in rage, "How dare you take photographs without my permission?"

I was about to say sorry, but he carried on saying, "How would you feel if somebody invaded your kitchen without your permission and started interfering? You just came in and started clicking as if this was a museum. You should have asked for my permission."

Although his tone became a bit milder, he still looked upset. He adjusted his spectacles and wiped the sweat from his forehead with the red scarf that he was wearing around his neck. He opened the curtain again. I was at a loss for words as I realised my mistake. I had really upset him, though subconsciously. I didn't know what to say. Although I was wrong, I couldn't fathom the way he shouted at me. There was no sign anywhere in the vicinity that prohibited photography.

For a second, I thought, "Sod the tour." I kept calm until the other devotee left. I made another mistake by telling the priest exactly what I thought of his outburst.

I said to him, "Panditji! You seemed to be very arrogant and intolerant. This is not your kitchen but a place of worship where anybody can come to pray. I am sorry for my mistake, but you are a short-tempered priest."

I immediately realised that I shouldn't have said anything that would upset him. He was not only a priest but also a highly respected gentleman who was manning one of the most historical temples.

I registered my apology again and said, "I didn't mean to be rude, but on the spur of the moment, I couldn't digest the fact that I would not be able to pay my obeisance and take any photograph of such a significant place after travelling this far."

He mellowed his voice and said, "I didn't mean to hurt you. I hope you understand."

I could see a genuine smile on his face.

"My voice is a bit too loud, but peace and dignity of the place have to be maintained," he carried on saying while asking us to sit in front of the deities.

It was a great relief. He prayed for us, and we paid our obeisance to the Gods.

In fact, he was a very nice person with a great knowledge of history. He asked us to follow him to the adjoining shrine in the same temple. Intrigued, I obeyed him. This section of the shrine felt like a haven of peace infused with the spirituality of religious devotion. He asked me to look carefully and discreetly at the statue on a platform. It was a statue of Goswami Tulsi Das that was dressed in golden yellow attire. It looked as if Tulsi Das had been meditating for years. But what was extraordinary about it was that it resembled the photograph of Tulsi Das. The face was shining gracefully.

Panditji told us the history and mythical facts related to Tulsi's statue, which was recovered from the riverbed. It seemed Panditji had shown us a trailer of one of the incidents that took place during the 16th century.

He lifted the statue of Tulsi Das from the dais and began to undo the outfit. As he took off the layers, an amazing two-foot-tall stone in ash black colour was in his hands. It was in a sitting posture. It looked glossy black above the waist, as if the priest had been applying some oil on the upper part of the body every day, and it looked very dull below the waistline. The watermark on the waist was conspicuous. It seemed that the statue must have been in the water for a long period of time before it was recovered. I jokingly asked Panditji if I could take a photograph. He raised his grey eyebrows and negated my request with a smile. Panditji was so kind that he allowed me to hold the statue of Tulsi Das. I gently and respectfully put my hands beneath the statue and held it steady for a few seconds. It felt like a balm to the soul, especially after the first incident. I felt honoured and thanked him from the core of my heart.

Panditji told us the story of the statue of Tulsi Das in a nutshell while adorning it. Apparently, it was found on the bed of the Yamuna River near this place.

I respectfully asked the priest's permission to treasure some memories of Tulsi Kuteer in the form of photographs. He not only allowed me to go ahead but also directed me patiently to click my camera from the right spot. At this juncture, I didn't regret that little stint in the beginning as I saw some positive outcomes.

The priest eventually introduced himself as Pandit Onkar Nath Chaturvedi. His generation was the eleventh in the lineage of Pandit Ganpati Upadhyay, who was the disciple of Tulsi Das. He also told us to visit Prabhu ghat where Rama, Sita, and Lakshmana crossed the Yamuna to reach Chitrakoot. He also asked me to write some views in the visitor's book; I felt honoured and wrote how I felt. It was my great privilege to interact with a person of such calibre.

The cool breeze was blowing outside the temple; it felt more soothing after the unnecessary heated argument. We were joined by another priest, Pandit Ramashraya Tripathi, who was also the eleventh generation in the lineage of the same disciple of Tulsi Das; he was manning another famous temple, Maanas Mandir, that was tucked away in the corner near the car park. Panditji looked over 6 feet tall, with a long grey beard. He was very cool and composed. We followed him to Maanas Mandir. Panditji took us to the room adjoining Maanas Mandir; it was a clean, small room; the colourful carpet suited the place.

Pandit Tripathi ji asked us to sit on the floor while taking a large bunch of keys out of the side pocket of his shirt. He was the custodian of the Ayodhya Kanda, the original manuscript of The Ramayana. He opened a large steel safe that was fixed in the wall. It was a moment of excitement, but I tried to keep calm and composed.

Panditji began to brief us as soon as he opened the safe; he bowed respectfully and brought out the original manuscript of Ayodhya Kanda wrapped in many layers of different pieces of cloth. He placed it on the clean sheet in the middle of the room. He showed us the original pages of Ayodhya Kanda; each page was wrapped separately for their protection. Panditji Tripathi ji not only had a comprehensive collection of history wrapped in layers of velvet but also kept it magnificently intact and secured in the safe. He was kind enough to let us hold some of the pages. I respectfully bowed and gently touched them. It was like going into The Ramayana era and touching the holy feet of Lord Rama. I felt privileged; it was like a dream come true. He shared extensive knowledge about the epic and original writing style in Awadhi. He explained how the changes have taken place in writing Hindi in recent times and the time of this manuscript. He kept us engrossed for a considerable time.

As Panditji came out to see us off, I mentioned the book I am writing. I was pleased beyond words when he asked me to donate a copy of my book to their collection of books when it is published.

After exploring all the sites in the periphery of Chitrakoot, I found it to be one of my favourite places.

Postscript – One day, during the coronavirus period, I received a call from Pandit Onkar Nath Chaturvedi ji. It was my pleasure to converse with him. He sounded very concerned about the health and welfare of the local monkeys. He asked me to help as there were no pilgrims to support them. I was happy to oblige, and we kept in touch with each other for a long time. One day, his son conveyed the message of his demise. I felt as if I had lost one of my family members.

Now, I keep in touch with Pandit Tripathi ji and get updates about the developments of the temple premises.

NASHIK CIRCUIT

It was still dark when the driver pulled up in his seven-seater taxi, a Toyota Innova, to pick us up from the guesthouse in Vashi, Navi Mumbai. He handed over a container of parathas and snacks that were sent by Raman Saily, a family friend. We began our maiden journey from Navi Mumbai to Nashik at 6.30 am. Although rail and bus options were widely available, we decided to hire a taxi as it was the most convenient way for 6 people – Ashok and Indu from Gateshead, Yogesh and Tripta from London, and Janak and I – to travel comfortably.

I was so nervous, as well as thrilled about this trip, that I hardly slept a wink the previous night. My anxiety was natural as it was my first mission to explore the significant sites related to The Ramayana. An unabridged itinerary was dancing before my eyes. But as I thought about the spiritual sites, my edginess evaporated.

The men in the back seat were busy telling tales, and the ladies went into slumber mode. I kept my eyes on the road while talking to the driver about the lives of taxi drivers and their families. Soon after, I could hear some unromantic tunes coming from Yogesh's nostrils. He was well and truly in the land of dreams.

As the road became clearer, the driver hurtled along at speed, wildly overtaking many trucks and cars. It seemed he was under the influence of Formula One driver Michael Schumacher as he drove at breakneck speed on the dual carriageway, but, thankfully, with enviable skill and care.

Gazing around, I saw some rugged hills and realised the city of Nashik was drawing near. At first glance, the scenery did not look as majestic, but as we headed towards the city, its serenity allured me;

the lush green valley in the distance and some vegetation groves were eye-catching.

Historically ancient, yet thoroughly modern and industrious, Nashik is a vibrant city surrounded by 9 splendid hills. It is dotted with a significant number of lush green farms and the River Godavari that runs through the city.

No one knows when the city of Nashik came into existence. From archaeological excavations, it was discovered that the territory around Nashik was occupied in the early Stone Age. It is claimed that the renowned sage Agastya was the first Aryan to cross the Vindhya Mountains and live on the banks of the Godavari. Truly, Nashik has a personality of its own because of its mythological, historical, social, and cultural importance. As it is situated along the river Godavari, it is considered one of the holiest places for Hindus all over the world.

PROMINENT SITES IN AND AROUND NASHIK

Coming back to the prime reason for my visit, Nashik was the place where the hero of The Ramayana, Rama, Sita, and Lakshman, made their abode during their exile of 14 years; they spent a year and a half around here. According to mythology, it was here that Lakshmana cut off the nose of Surpnakha, the sister of the demon king Ravana. Hence, the city earned the name Nashik. This is a city that houses some of the most revered temples and monuments from The Ramayana era. Its powerful history has inspired many educational institutions to teach Puranas, Vedas, Numismatic Studies, and several other related courses that are not available anywhere else in the country.

After a long drive, and that too without breakfast, everybody felt the need for some nutrition. We came down into the breakfast hall and asked for some cutlery needed for our home-cooked potato-stuffed parathas and yogurt. Lime and mango pickles were there to spice up the taste. Yogesh asked the waiter to bring 6 cups of tea straight away, and 6 cups after 20 minutes, as he preferred hot tea to yogurt with parathas.

Tripta commented, "Rama Saily and her daughter-in-law, Ritu, must be up at 4 o'clock to make so many parathas."

"Maybe they're very good cooks though, you can surely taste the difference between the hotel food and the one prepared at home," Janak joined the conversation while washing down the food with a sip of tea.

Fortunately, it was a beautiful, sunny late morning, and I was ready to launch my itinerary for the day.

"Will it be a good omen if we begin our tour from Rama Ghat, being the most sacred point in Nashik?" I asked the driver.

"Yes, I think so," he readily agreed.

RAMA GHAT

As we reached the main square in the old city, there were ample spaces in the car park near the Ganga Godavari temple. We chose to walk everywhere around the ghats and the vicinity of Panchvati, an important site during The Ramayana era.

As they say, every expedition needs an expert, so I hired a guide for the right information.

The lanky old man cheerfully said, "You have picked the right time of the day because, after the morning rush, the number of devotees thins out. Late morning is the best time to explore the ghats and temples in relative solitude for a couple of hours."

The guide affirmed that the most important place in Nasik was the complex of Panchvati on the banks of the Godavari. Therefore, we inaugurated our tour from Panchvati's Rama Kund, meaning a small holy well.

The Rama Kund is in the river Godavari and draws innumerable pilgrims every year. As the river Godavari takes a right-angled turn to the south from this very point, it is considered the most holy corner by the pilgrims. It is believed that Lord Rama and his consort, Sita, bathed here during their exile. To commemorate that gesture, pilgrims frequently take a dip in this holy well. The Godavari River is also considered the 'Ganges of the south'.

The guide led us towards Rama Kund, where the atmosphere was very spiritual. We started our pilgrimage with a holy dip in the Kund. I went into the water and washed my face; I considered it my first blessing. Lots of ladies were praying while dipping in the murky waters to my right. Some offerings, such as leaves or marigolds, were floating near the steps, and young children were splashing the water all around.

There was another reason why this place was considered so sacred. In Hindu culture, when the body is cremated after death, the ashes are then scattered in the sacred water. It is believed that Rama Kund has internal natural water springs which help to dissolve the bones and ashes easily.

The next morning, Janak and I decided to go there to cherish the atmosphere. We performed the necessary rituals and took a holy dip, which is considered most auspicious when taken in the morning. I didn't want to miss any of such opportunities, so I tried to recite some of the mantras while standing in the knee-deep holy waters. My wife seemed quite impressed with this specific act of praying, and she asked, 'What were you murmuring?' I just laughed...

After sunset, it appeared most of the pilgrims were flooding towards the riverside for the evening aarti. Young and old priests conducted the aarti with full vigour. Some of them had sweat pouring down behind their ears, but their faces were aglow with reverence. I thoroughly enjoyed the sounds of rhythmic drum beating.

Giving alms to the needy is said to bring good luck. There was no dearth of people who would gladly accept the alms in any form. Two girls, aged between 11 and 13, chased us for some money. I agreed to buy some food instead of giving money. They cutely asked me to buy some Chinese noodles instead of local food. When they got their dish on the table in the open courtyard, their faces lit up. They grabbed their cutlery in a flash and tried to pick up the noodles by turning and twisting the fork. They looked around shyly and quickly discarded the cutlery on the side and began to relish the food with their hands. The smile on their faces was clear in any language.

After having some sins wiped off the slate, we went to the Ganga Godavari temple to seek more blessings for a safe and sound trip ahead.

KALA RAMA TEMPLE

On a glorious late morning, with the mercury hovering around the 30°C mark, we walked towards the famous temple of Kala Rama which was just round the corner. As soon as we entered the precinct, I noticed the temple was well-maintained. Being on the banks of a river, I was expecting it to be full of mud, sand, or dirt, but it was very clean. The idols of Rama, Sita, Lakshmana, and Hanuman were black; these are said to be self-manifested.

As we stepped into a long 40-pillared corridor, an idol of black Hanuman was positioned at the front, facing the main sanctum. Our guide advised us to chant Hanuman Chalisa and not to look back while walking towards the Kala Rama shrine. The 40 pillars represented the 40 shlokas of Hanuman Chalisa. I could feel a religious atmosphere all around.

After passing through the veranda, we entered the main shrine, where the deities were enshrined on a raised platform. Interestingly, there were 14 steps to reach the temple gate, representing Lord Rama's 14 years in exile. The red and gold outfits enhanced the beauty of the idols.

As we came out, a small platform under the cluster of trees proved to be a boon for the aching knees. A man, with an untidy beard and a red scarf on his head, was roasting some fresh corn on the cob on the open charcoal fire. Everyone followed me to taste one. That was a nice break before heading to the Sita Gufa.

SITA GUFA AND PANCHVATI

The Sita Gufa played a pivotal role in the text of The Ramayana. It was a stone's throw from the Kala Rama Temple and in the same holy precinct of Panchvati. Once stood by the riverside, this sacred spot of Panchvati got its name from the '5 Banyan trees'. 'Panch' means 5, and 'vati' means Banyan tree. But now, due to encroachment and development by the local authorities, the river has been pushed back a good few metres away from this iconic site.

As we were strolling towards the Sita Gufa, we came across a few grazing cows jostling for space or looking for fodder in the middle of the road, but we negotiated our way across. Just around the corner, a heaving group of pilgrims was chanting prayers and some religious songs in a regional language while swaying their hands high in the air. We quickly squeezed through them all and went towards the famous Gufa. There were few pilgrims at this time of the day as the school and college exams were in full swing.

Sita Gufa is believed to be the place where Sita once took refuge when Rama went to catch a deer at her insistence. This was the very place where Sita was kidnapped by King Ravana. According to mythology, when Rama and Lakshmana were away to catch the golden deer, an image of Sita herself arose from the kitchen fire of Sita's hermitage. She said to Sita, "You enter the fire and live with the fire God until the demise of Ravana, and I will take your place." Sita agreed. Hence, Ravana ended up kidnapping Sita's image, assuming she was the real Sita.

The main cave complex on the ground level has some murals depicting the main incidents involving the kidnapping of Sita. The scenes of Maricha's killing, the Lakshmana-Rekha, and Sita's kidnapping adorned the colourful walls.

As we entered the vestibule of the Gufa, there was hardly anyone around. A couple of people were inquiring about some souvenirs on the counter in the corner. Although every one of us wanted to go down into the cave, none of us was prepared to venture out to lead the group or even showed the courage. The cave was accessible through a narrow staircase, and only one person at a time could go down. I must confess, initially, I was nervous about going down to the constricted cave, and then I tried to calm myself down by looking at the murals on the walls and gathered some courage from within. I didn't show anxiety on my face and categorically told my companions to follow me.

In excitement or rather nervousness, I banged my head while entering the cave and got a little bump on the forehead. I crossed my fingers while sliding down the steps. There was no idol or statue of any God inside the landing cave, yet it was considered very sacred. The sandstone interior walls and a small doorway to the adjoining caves were cleverly built. It looked safe and sound. Just to counter my claustrophobia, I prayed to Lord Hanuman to get myself some strength and hastened to pay obeisance to the idols. The deities of Rama, Sita, and Lakshmana were placed in the first main Gufa, and in the small adjoining cave, the Shiva Lingam was enshrined. It is believed that this was the same Shiva Lingam that Sita worshipped during her stay. At times, I felt I would like to go out and get some fresh air, but instead, I massaged my throbbing temples a couple of times to concentrate. Thankfully, the cave had a separate entrance and exit. I hastened my way out and felt relieved to see the daylight again. However, I would not recommend this visit to pilgrims of a nervous disposition, especially during the festive days. But my wife had no apprehension and felt quite comfortable. As soon as we came out, she squinted and just laughed. It was no surprise because she is more adventurous than I am. The same thing happened to my other male friends, who breathed a sigh of relief as they came out, but their spouses felt comfortable. I wondered how different this structure was from the original cave, and I could never imagine what it really looked like during Rama's stay. Nevertheless, it was a satisfying experience overall.

The crowd of pilgrims began to swell by the time we came out of the Sita Gufa. We immediately went to another temple, Gora Rama, across the road. There wasn't anything major to see except a few murals on the walls depicting some incidents of Ramayana. However, 5 Banyan trees in the same vicinity added to the beauty and charm of the whole Panchvati area. Three of them were clustered next to the cave, and 2 graced the site across the road. Some carefree people were sitting and gossiping on the platforms made at the base of the trees. I was so intrigued by the Gufa and the 5 trees that I thought I was witnessing a historic moment. What struck me the most was not how magnificent the Kala Rama Temple, Sita Gufa, or the 5 Banyan trees were but how intact and glorious they remained after so many years.

Occasionally, the guide behaved like a train engine on a fixed route - just follow me, listen to me, and no questions asked. Ashok was probably still admiring the vicinity or was in a world of his own; he could not understand what the guide said about Panchvati. So, he interrupted his continuous commentary and asked him to speak slowly. At times, his whistling speech, due to some missing front teeth, was hard to grasp. At this point, the guide lost his temper and said in a loud voice, 'Don't you understand Hindi? Where have you come from?' Initially, we burst into peals of laughter over his outburst but then ignored his remarks to ward off any imminent trouble. He was a good guide but a bit of 'do lalli'. However unfair it may seem, I decided to terminate his services and continue our trip.

Panchvati was an intriguing mixture of loud and quiet. The hustle and bustle of pilgrims, shopkeepers, and hawkers was clearly audible. But in contrast, the religious shrines provided a great tranquillity. Some shops selling DVDs and related products were playing religious songs to the Bollywood tunes, while pilgrims bought souvenirs. Certainly, there was plenty to see, but my energy level was depleted by the end.

I told them while patting my potbelly, "My stomach will revolt if we do not stop for a meal."

They all agreed, and we decided to go for a South Indian dish - Masala Dosa. The meal turned out to be a lengthy affair but sumptuous. After a refreshing cup of tea, we decided to move on.

In the old city, 2 and three-wheelers were often seen travelling against the flow of traffic, paying little heed to recently added road signs or speed breakers. But we had the advantage of having our own vehicle. Some tender-coconut slices from the roadside hawker looked quite refreshing; I had more than everyone else.

TAPOVAN

Tapovan literally means a precinct reserved for meditation and penance. Once on the fringe of the Dandakaranya forest, it was a picturesque spot rich in greenery. It offered the perfect combination of total relaxation, tranquillity, and seclusion, as well as filling a day with various religious activities.

As we pulled up at an unpaved and untidy car park, I asked the driver to arrange for an experienced guide for us. Though there has been a lot of industrial growth in the vicinity, this was still the place where history, mythology, and religion were very much honoured and followed. Tapovan has a special place in the heart of every Hindu as the pivotal and watershed incident of The Ramayana, chopping off Surpnakha's nose, took place at this very spot.

Lakshmana built 2 Parnakutis - cottages - in the forest; one for Rama and Sita and the other one for himself. Their entourage went through several absorbing experiences. A disaster struck during their last year and a half in exile when Surpnakha became attracted to Rama's charming personality, and Rama rejected her advances. She then turned to his brother, Lakshmana, but he ridiculed her. Surpnakha felt insulted and tried to malign Sita. Lakshmana couldn't bear her being rude to Sita, and in a fit of rage, he cut off Surpnakha's nose and ears.

Our guide, a charming young man, greeted us with a traditional 'Namaste' and a handshake. He said, "The Godavari's gurgling stream and the stunning landscape enthral the pilgrim's mind. The historical sites and the wild, untamed scenery of Tapovan draw pilgrims and tourists from all over India and beyond."

He continued, "I want you to have a true picture of the history and the real feelings of the incidents that took place during Rama's exile."

He started with the temple next to the car park. The small but clean temple under a fascinating Banyan tree graced Lakshmana's only significant shrine in India.

I interrupted the guide and said, "I have visited another Lakshmana temple at Hem Kund Sahib in Uttarakhand, in the vicinity of the Gurudwara."

He did not know anything about that temple. Anyhow, he took us to another small temple of Sheshnaga, the King of Serpents, the seat of Lord Vishnu, who was reincarnated as Lakshmana. Nearby, the most important temple, where Lakshmana is said to have cut off Surpnakha's nose, was situated. We climbed a few steps to reach the temple, where a statue of Lakshmana chopping off Surpnakha's nose was placed.

Sadly, it did not look elaborate; it was just a simple statue exhibiting the incident. The temple authorities were drumming up financial support from the pilgrims to construct a huge Lakshmana temple. We paid our obeisance. I took my time and adored the serenity of the environment.

As we proceeded, we came across another prominent shrine of Rama and Sita; it was believed to be Rama's cottage. The priest of the temple explained the importance of this place. Lakshmana used to bring some water from the river and logs from the forest while Sita cooked the meals.

It gave me some discomfort to see that such a renowned shrine was tucked away in an ordinary manner. These unique monuments and historical structures needed an immediate facelift.

The priest said while walking along, "We are going to build an opulent temple and develop this area as an exemplary Hindu pilgrim destination, but we need some magnanimous donors."

It required some special attention to renovate temples that were wallowing in neglect or eroding with age. The sanitation facilities were almost non-existent, and whatever was provided, it looked rather scant and non-functional.

While strolling around the precinct, we gently wound our way to the confluence where the Godavari and Kapila rivers were flowing together. The setting of the rivers and the rocks amidst greenery looked impeccable. An arc bridge and the statues of Rama, Sita, and Lakshmana, carved out of iron, on a small hill enhanced the beauty of the surroundings. We took a little break and enjoyed some home-made creamy ice cream served on a banana leaf. It reminded me of my childhood when I used to wait for an ice cream vendor who used to bring the same kind of ice cream container and used to give only a thin layer on the leaf.

I was keen to ask our guide about the small wells in the rocks which were surrounded by a few pilgrims near the confluence of the rivers. He just laughed and said, "These are not ordinary ponds of water, they are called Tirthas. The first one is called Brahma Tirtha, the second one is Shiva Tirtha, and the next one is known as Vishnu Tirtha."

Suddenly, everyone looked keen to follow where the guide was pointing. There were a few more Kund around. These differently sized ponds, less than one metre wide and 2 metres in length, were full of clean greenish water. Surprisingly, they were linked to each other from the bottom by narrow paths. Sage Kapila is believed to have meditated here. Therefore, one of them was called Kapila Tirtha where his name was carved on a rock near the edge of a pond.

While moving to the left, the guide explained, "This is a very significant Kund, known as Agni-tirtha. This is the deepest one among all the ponds. Rama had asked Sita to sit here while keeping the image of Sita with him. So, only the image of Sita was later abducted by Ravana from Sita Gufa."

He told us the story of 'Lilla', relating to Sita's chastity test when Sita had to walk through the flames of the pyre.

A lady who was following our guide could not understand what he was saying. She said to her friend, "I think this young man does not know much about this place; he is just confusing everyone."

Everyone raised their eyebrows while looking discreetly around the pond.

It was mind-boggling to think how Sita could have been kept in a small area or how her image accompanied Rama. However, it was fascinating to know the historical facts, and I felt pleased in my heart; I was living the glorious past.

At first glance, it looked like there wasn't much to see, but when I realised its importance in the context of the whole historical site, I was amazed. The framework of the temples and the spots where various incidents took place were still evident, and I could visualise what it would have been like thousands of years ago.

The small rocky area looked clean and attractive, but I felt unsafe around the tanks as there were no railings or any other kind of protection. It must be dangerous during the festive days when the crowds are in thousands and the rocks could be slippery.

Surprisingly, after so many years of wind and rain erosion, the tanks and confluence still make for a spectacular landscape. Nearby, a small wooden arch bridge enhances the beauty. An attractive setting of a natural mound of rocks between the river and the greenery forced me to take a little break.

Tapovan was more endearing and greener than in the history books. I could never imagine what it was like during the era when Rama was in exile, but I could certainly visualise that the essence of The Ramayana was sown here.

KISHKINDHA AND HAMPI

We reached Hampi late in the evening, so we had a quick dinner at the hotel. I snuggled between the sheets by 9.30 pm, but I was unable to sleep. I kept staring at the ceiling while my brain wandered somewhere else. When I glanced across at the clock on the table, it was past midnight. I wanted to drift off, but the aspiration of exploring Kishkindha, the land of Gods, kept my mind racing at 100 kmph. Nonetheless, after an anxious night, I was up in time for the morning tour. The buffet breakfast made me feel as fresh as ever.

The moment I set foot on the land of 'ancient ruins', I was mesmerised. I immediately perceived that I was somewhere spectacular. I was overwhelmed when I gazed around. There were randomly scattered huge mountains of honey-coloured boulders, tall temple towers, historical monuments, and cultivated fields of green paddy dotted with palm trees right in front of my eyes. All my preconceived visions were thrown out of the window. It seemed impossible to separate the World Heritage Site of Hampi from mythical Kishkindha.

The whole area had an atmosphere of stillness. A rapid transition from imagination to reality shook my senses; it unfolded so much and so easily. If you think time travel is a myth, think again, rev up your time machine and travel back in time to the capital of the forgotten empire.

HISTORY OF HAMPI

Millions of years ago, there were no boulders on the surface of Hampi. The wind and rain had continuously swept away the soft soil, exposing the hard rocky outcrop. In fact, what you see in Hampi is one of the oldest surfaces one can see on Earth. Thanks to the elements and the fault lines on these rocky surfaces, cracks appeared, and the never-ending formation of boulders began. The natural erosion polished the boulders into bizarre shapes. Unlike how pebbles are polished in the flowing water of the river, Hampi boulders were formed by blowing winds. The strongly blowing sand was something like rubbing a hard surface with sandpaper. This continued for many thousands of years, crafting the landscape of Hampi. The result is a mysterious-looking landscape, as if God had emptied the bags of boulders over Hampi.

In ancient times, Hampi was known by several names such as Pampa-kshetra and Kishkindha-kshetra. It is believed that the first historical settlements in Hampi date back to the beginning of the Central Era. The seat of the Vijayanagara Empire was established by Saint Vijaya Ranga in 1336 CE with the help of 2 of his disciples, Hakka and Bakka. The empire became a prosperous and wealthy kingdom within a short span of time. The kingdom flourished under the rule of Emperor Krishnadeva Raya, and it reached its peak. Hampi was the capital of the largest empire in post-Mughal India, from 1343 to 1565. This period witnessed a resurgence of the Hindu religion, art, and architecture on an unprecedented scale.

Hampi became renowned because of its immense wealth and flourishing business, trading in a wide variety of items from horses to gems. The temples of Hampi were noted for their large dimensions, florid ornamentation, bold and delicate carvings, stately pillars, magnificent pavilions, and a great wealth of traditional depictions including subjects from the epics Ramayana and Mahabharata.

The warring Deccan sultanates finally joined together and defeated Vijaynagara's army at Talari Kota, a place north of Hampi. Soon after the demise of the kings, the Bahamani Sultans looted the kingdom and ransacked its palaces and temples. It is believed that it took more than 6 months to destroy the historical monuments, and they used more than a hundred elephants to transport the precious treasure.

For centuries, Hampi continued as a neglected place. This erstwhile metropolitan slowly turned into a jungle. During the colonial period, Hampi evoked more curiosity among the western archaeologists. Robert

Sewell's seminal work aptly titled 'A Forgotten Empire Vijayanagar' was a major attempt to narrate the empire that was. Then, Hampi was an irrelevant and graceless town, but it narrated an ancient history which no other place in India could match. Now, this was a town touched by tourism rather than changed by it.

Soon, the area of Hampi began to become a haven for European travellers who were lured by unparalleled picture-perfect landscapes and unspoilt rural life. Then, it was also associated with the pseudo-hippie crowd and late-night parties. Eventually, it was granted the status of a World Heritage Site by UNESCO in 1996.

HEMAKUTA HILL AND VIRUPAKSA TEMPLE

This once-forgotten area became the region to be explored, thanks to the mythology and history. We started the day from Hemakuta hill, which was on the southern side of the village, Kamlapur. It was almost a flat expanse of rocky sheet with occasional ups and downs. As our Toyota Innova Taxi reached the summit, the panorama unfolded below. It overlooked the sacred centre, offering a splendid view of the sprawling ruin site. The Virupaksa temple on the left was the highlight of the vista. The Tungabhadra River to its north looked serene.

The whole area was dotted with ancient temples and clusters of shrines. On the opposite side, a sea of banana plantations swamped the land up to the base of the boulder hills.

Most of the temples on the Hemakuta hill were dedicated to Lord Shiva and his family. Some of the temples were partially sunk into the ground. An idol of Ganesha, a monolithic sculpture, looked fascinating in one of the temples. Since there were far fewer fellow tourists on the hill, we simply enjoyed the relatively calm atmosphere.

The descending road led to the main bazaar in front of the Virupaksha temple. It felt good as I was walking on a glorious past, once the bustling market and the soul of Hampi.

The towering nine-story gopuram of Virupaksa temple greeted us. The architecture on the temple gate and the walls looked awe-inspiring with details of the mythological scenes and the images of the various Gods. It was dedicated to Lord Shiva. This was the only temple in the area that was still in use, although there were several dilapidated mandapas in the vicinity.

The central Mandapa was a most ornate structure. Some ancient inscriptions, which dated back to the ninth century, looked as if they were fading away. The statue of a black Nandi bull in a sitting posture was the best in the complex. As I strolled leisurely in the open courtyard, I encountered a few cheeky monkeys but was saved from trouble by throwing some food and 2 halves of coconut across the wall. One of them kept looking at me, his eyeballs moving fast from left to right while stuffing his face with young coconut out of the shell.

As we went further on past a banana plantation, we saw a giant and impressive statue of Narsimha, the incarnation of Vishnu, adorning the small open temple. In the same vicinity, a huge Shiv-lingam was housed in a small closet with its base permanently underwater. It is said to have been commissioned by a poor woman who used her life savings to pay for it.

VITHALA TEMPLE

It was time to witness the focal point of Hampi, the Vithala temple. To get under the skin of the place, I hired a guide. As we travelled, I was constantly intrigued by the boulder-hill landscape and the rocks precariously perched on top of each other. I could visualise the place in its glory days, and my mischievous mind kept me busy by making imaginary figures from the variety of stones along the way.

It was a warm morning, but a pleasant breeze wafting from the Tungabhadra River took some of the sting out of the hot sun. The road leading to the temple was very wide but in a bad state; it was dusty and uneven. I didn't want to walk down the spooky, rough, sunken path, so we took a ride on an electric auto-buggy.

The ruins of the once-vast market known as Vithala Bazaar were evident on either side of the road. It was no ordinary bazaar; it was famous for trading horses and other valuable products, including rubies, diamonds, and pearls. Literally, I was walking in the footprints of mighty kings where priceless treasures were sold in measures. The architecture on the ruined pillars on both sides bore the marks of Hampi's many conquerors.

The long and wide street led to the stunning sight of the towering gateway of the Vithala temple. My eyes examined the ruins of Pushkarni on the right before entering the monumental place. I yelled to myself, "I knew a bit of the history of the cruel and insensitive Mughals, but I never thought they would have lost their minds for materialistic gains to that extent." Their greed was conspicuous.

The Vithala temple was dedicated to Lord Vishnu in his Vithala form. It was the largest temple built by Devaraya 2 in the Dravidian style of architecture. The images of the temple depicted the true intentions behind the empire's encouragement for art and music.

The temple complex was a sprawling area surrounded by high compound walls and 3 towering gateways that had been eroded by the passage of time. Vithala must be the grandest of all the temples in Hampi. It exemplified the immense creativity and architectural excellence possessed by the sculptures and artisans of the Vijayanagar Empire.

I began by visualising the Maha Mandapa - the main open hall. It was positioned on a highly ornate base that was decorated with carvings of warriors, horses, and many ornamental designs. The Mandapa was comprised of 4 smaller halls, and its 40 pillars lined the facade of the temple. The central rectangular courtyard, with 16 intricately carved pillars, had beautiful sculptures of Narsimha. A criss-crossed marble net formed a ceiling which was richly designed and carved.

Next, I walked in the middle of the complex where a massive stone chariot was placed. It looked awe-inspiring under the shining rays of the sun. An extravaganza in stone was the most stunning piece of architecture of Vijayanagar. It had a special feel as it was a shrine that had been designed in the shape of an ornamental chariot. The shrine was dedicated to Garuda, the vehicle of Lord Vishnu. Relatively, this place has withstood the ravages of man and time.

The stone wheels of the Rath were once functional and could be rotated by people. The chariot was placed on a richly sculpted base that was supported by some shafts which were carved out of a single stone. It was a breathless marvel of stone architecture where time seemed to stand still. Witnessing the history was worth the trip alone.

Then, I moved towards another magnetic site, Ranjha Mandapa, renowned for its 56 musical pillars. In the contemporary world, these pillars are also known as SA-RE-GA-MA pillars, indicating the musical notes emitted by them. They still emanate when the pillars are tapped gently. It appeared that every monument had more details of art and carvings than the previous one. There were carvings on the base of the temple that represented images of some foreigners trading horses.

In the extensive hall, there was a set of main pillars that provided support to the ceiling. Amazingly, each one was carved as a musical instrument and was surrounded by 7 minor pillars. These emit 7 different musical notes which vary in sound quality depending on whether the instrument was a percussion, string, or wind instrument; each musical pillar was carved out of a single piece of resonant stone. Our guide tapped them professionally and showed us how they worked. He asked me to try it out. After repeated attempts, a sound was produced, but there was no rhythm at all.

"Probably, I need a few years of experience," I said to the guide. He turned his head halfway around, smirked, and gave me a satirical look.

Apparently, the emission of notes from musical pillars was a mystery that fascinated many people, including the British rulers of India. They were wonderstruck and wanted to discover the secret behind it. To satisfy their curiosity, the British authorities ordered that 2 of the pillars should be cut to reveal whether anything existed inside them that resulted in the emission of musical notes. Evidently, they found nothing inside them, and the broken remains are still in the hall.

I was astonished at every site. They had different styles of architecture but held the same intrigue. The main temple in the complex was partially ruined; the sanctum sanctorum, once graced with an idol of Lord Vithala, was devoid of any idol. The western hall was spoiled long ago during the attack by the Mughals that led to the fall of the empire. It was a place to cause heartbreak.

The exceptional architecture and craftsmanship on every stone seemed to be saying in silence, 'Why are you murmuring and groaning now? Where were you and your ancestors, and their appreciation when the obnoxious devils were thrashing us?'

I wasn't sure whether I was encouraged or baffled by the monotony of the seemingly endless stretch of the landscapes, but I certainly enjoyed the extraordinary rock formation that inspired several sets of imaginary scenes.

After walking around all day, my sore and tired muscles appreciated the pleasure of having a bath in the warm water. I slept like a baby for the rest of the night.

THE ROYAL ENCLOSURE

Dawn broke on yet another blissful day. I loaded as many calories as I could, knowing well that my next dose would surely be at lunchtime. We were on the track for our next mission, the Royal Enclosure and its surrounding area.

We started with a secluded area reserved for the royal ladies. In most of the historical cities in Europe, there would be long queues for tickets, and these would cost exorbitant prices, but here, we paid a nominal amount for the entry ticket at the door and were soon inside the complex.

The entire area was covered with monuments and stone structures showcasing the elaborate layout that bore testimony to the architectural perfection of the master craftsmen of the era. Every nook and corner that I discovered had some sort of history woven into it.

The Zenana Enclosure was fortified by tall walls and a watchtower. Some of the walls looked as if they were crumbling. The huge stone foundation of the Queen's Palace in the compound on the left depicted the extraordinary wealth of the Vijayanagar Empire. The splendid remains of the magnificent palace and the destruction inflicted by the Mughals were visible. Huge halls, large rooms, and thick walls were full of charisma. It retained the footprints of its past. In a way, it was a depiction of how the royals lived. The sadness of this elegant palace was offset by the sheer beauty of its stonework and architecture. It was laden with symbolism. I was witnessing the palace where once the magnificent sparkle of the chandeliers used to charm the household but now, I had to make do with the silent glittering sunshine on the ruins.

Many school children in colourful outfits were roaming around the monuments. The teachers seemed to be briefing them in groups, and the sound of clicking cameras and the noise of merriment while posing for 'selfies' were evident.

I was searching for history, but again and again, I found myself distracted by some natural phenomenon. Not monkeys, but lizards this time, dashing for their crevices. My eyes followed one of them. The gap between the stones was too small to escape, but incredibly, she squeezed herself into a vertical long thin hollow line and disappeared. I noticed there were some insects playing hide and seek, or rather hide and run fast from the lizard; for the time being, their lives were spared.

We strolled towards the unblemished monument of Lotus Palace within a spectacular setting. It was striking with a great view of twin trees and lawns that sprang up around the Lotus Palace. The name was given because of the lotus motif on its arches, which were open on all sides for cool air.

The ornate structure of the Lotus Palace was probably used by the queens as a pleasure pavilion in summer. It was built with geometrical accuracy to ensure a perfect climate inside the structure. It was an old-style air-conditioned building where terracotta tiles ran through the walls, carrying cold water to cool off the place. The marvellous structure was dotted with numerous doors and windows.

We went further towards a small doorway that led us to the famous Elephant Stables, the shelter for the royal elephants. It was well-preserved. The enchanting sight of 10 domed stables transported me to its original era. The elegant structure was made of a series of chambers with dome-like roofs. Each chamber was big enough to accommodate 2 elephants and had a wooden beamed ceiling from which steel chains were attached to the elephants' necks and backs. The gracious, extra-wide buildings had an edge of grandeur entirely in keeping with the history.

As the sun was becoming brutal, a cluster of trees on the right proved to be a lifesaver. The value of a bottle of water was appreciated. Plenty of birds bobbing around the trees made the atmosphere a bit more soothing.

As we proceeded further, yet more architectural grandeur was in front of us. The Hazara Rama Temple, a private temple of the king, was compact and decorated with various carvings. The story of The Ramayana was impressively carved on all the shrine walls and columns, like comic strips on stone. The inner shrine contained 4 polished pillars with detailed carvings of religious themes.

I certainly needed to top up my sugar level, and my eyes needed a rest before I put them under stress again. The guide obliged with a smile. This restaurant was hidden behind the bushes; it was hard to figure out from the main road. When I came out of the taxi and turned right to follow others, I stood on a piece of dog's muck. As it was a dusty-muddy courtyard, I tried to clean it by rubbing my foot on loose dry soil and then knocked it off with the help of a stick from the bushes. Great start!

It was just like a small house in the village where most of the guests paused for lunch, sitting on scattered chairs, and then hurried on to wrap up their itinerary. Some hens, cocks, and rabbits ran haphazardly amid the jumble of uneven dining tables; the kud-kud of hens while chasing one another was fascinating. I just put my feet up on a small wooden stool and relaxed in the so-called garden restaurant with a refreshing swig of fresh orange juice. It was taking a long time to cook the fresh food, and I was enjoying the enforced siesta.

Soon after, I heard the sweet sound of a peacock. I thought I was dreaming, but I wasn't. A medium-sized peacock was running through the paddy fields that were a part of the restaurant's vicinity. I tried to capture him in my camera, but he was too quick for the lens. My food wasn't up to the mark, yet it was fresh enough for me to finish it off. A strong dose of caffeine opened my eyes for the next venture.

We moved on to the grandeur of the site of Disara Dibba – an elevated platform which was used during festivals or special occasions for the king to make public appearances. Although it didn't appear to be tall, the grand monument was visible from a distance.

It was too hot, so we moved further to admire the beauty of the ceremonial pond of the Queen's bath. An opulent squared stepped tank, made in a simple yet ascetic geometrical pattern, was another archaeological delight. This undamaged large bathing pool, made with brick-sized khaki stones, engaged many visitors who were taking photographs from every angle. The tank was connected to the aqueduct made by stone pillars. It showed how efficiently the water flowed from one place to another; it was amazing.

The Queen's bath looked like an indoor aquatic complex and was a perfect place for royals to bathe and relax. It was open to the sky but carefully shielded from all sides with the moat system to keep it cool for Her Highness. A large veranda with protruding Rajasthani balconies surrounding it glorified the central pool.

It was interesting to learn about the water system that filled the pool with fresh water. Two stone drains decorated with lion heads on one side of the pool were brilliantly mingled with the rest of the artwork; on another side, cool and perfumed water once poured in a small waterfall at one side and flowed out through the underground drains to the bath. To protect the royals from the sunshine, a small spot for an umbrella in the middle was visible. Another example of luxurious living was evident on the left where a large stone seat was erected for women servants who would shower rose petals and perfumed water on the royals while bathing. I stood in the corner and admired the immaculate engineering skills and masonry of the pool.

We were getting parched on the relentless journeys through the ancient ruins and temples, so fresh coconut water and a breather under the cluster of trees injected some energy. Tired legs at the end of the day were a small price to pay for exploring the splendid sites on foot.

It is believed in Hampi that 'anywhere you travel, history travels with you'; but here, history shakes your soul too. It was difficult to tell what was more charming in Hampi, its thrilling architecture or the bizarre-looking landscapes. The grandeur and crafted skill turned out to be on such a scale that it could dwarf many such sites in western cities. Generally, the ancient, ruined grandeurs of the world are compared with the Greek and Roman splendours, but after visiting here, one would certainly do the same for Hampi. On one hand, it was telling a tale of mankind's infinite talent and power of creativity and on the other, his capacity for senseless destruction. I wish a few Moguls were sensible like a German General Dietrich Von Choltitz who defied the orders of Hitler and refused to burn down Paris.

ANEGUNDI - KISHKINDHA

There was no dearth of history and mythology, and its importance related to The Ramayana. Even the founders of the Vijayanagar empire chose Hampi as a capital not only because it was a strategic point, the chain of boulder hills and the long and tempestuous Tungabhadra River making it a natural fortress, but also because their Gurus advised them of the spiritual powers of the entire region and emphasised the significance of Kishkindha that once flourished here. Kishkindha was the territory where less was more and more was meticulous. Kishkindha may not be a formal name now and is hence omitted from the map, but it is embossed in every Hindu's heart.

Anegundi has lingered in the shadow of Hampi. As I glanced through the history of Hampi, it gave way to stories of folklore and then proficiently sailed into mythology. Hampi and the surrounding villages have a strong historical and mythological association with the epic Ramayana, whose fourth chapter contains the story of Kishkindha. Anegundi, believed to be the citadel of the monkey kingdom of Kishkindha, was 5 kilometres from Hampi. All the sites around the area were part and parcel of The Ramayana trail. Anegundi's vast landscapes were said to be the kingdom of monkeys, which was ruled by King Bali. After killing Bali, the kingdom was handed over to his half-brother Sugreeva.

MONKEY KINGDOM

It is commonly held belief that the apes, also known as Vanaras, were a tribe of monkeys. Many historians believe that this is not the right interpretation of the word 'Vanaras' which literally translates to forest dwellers. It is derived from the Sanskrit word 'Van - Nar' which means 'forest-human'. They claim that the Vanaras were a human indigenous tribe of forest dwellers that lived during the time of The Ramayana. The whole region was within the dense forest called Dandakaranya forest extending from Vindhya Range to the South Indian peninsula. People coming from the north saw the Vanaras as not being human because they looked and behaved differently from themselves. Vanaras were, in fact, a human tribe that resembled the monkey. Hence, it is believed to be the kingdom of monkeys. Bali was the mighty king of this region.

It seemed a few travellers made it to Bali Parvat. It took less than half an hour from Kamlapur to reach the ancient citadel of Bali. It did not look different from other boulder hills but was quite spread around the bank of the Tungabhadra River. Inside the fort, a Durga temple was the highlight of the place. As the heat of the sun was at its peak, the decision to go for a quick lunch suited me fine.

It is believed that once, Dhundavi, the son of the demon Mayavi, arrived at Bali's door, drunk on the disillusioning power of his own strength. He shouted for Bali to fight with him. Dhundavi wanted to avenge the death of his father. Bali beat him up and sent him running in fear. Bali and his brother, Sugreeva, followed him to finish him off. But the demon ran into a cave.

Before running into the dark cave, Bali told Sugreeva, "If I do not come out by the end of one month, consider that I have been killed by Dhundavi."

After a month, Sugreeva saw a stream of blood flowing out of the cave. He thought his brother had been killed. Sugreeva placed a huge rock across the mouth of the cave so that it would be locked. The monkey clan persuaded him to take the place of Bali and much against his will, Sugreeva was crowned the king of Kishkindha. Meanwhile, Bali had killed the demon and when he tried to come out of the cave, he found the exit was blocked with a massive rock. Somehow, he managed to move the rock and reached Kishkindha. When he saw Sugreeva seated on the throne, his anger knew no bounds. He leapt at Sugreeva to kill him. He thought Sugreeva had deliberately blocked the mouth of the cave. Sugreeva took to his heels and ran for his life. Wherever he ran, Bali just followed him. Hanuman suggested to him that he should go to Rishyamuk Parvat where Bali would not climb as he was cursed by Sage Matanga.

HISTORY OF ANEGUNDI

The picturesque hamlet of Anegundi, perched on the banks of the River Tungabhadra, is steeped in mythology and history. It is said to have one of the oldest plateaus on the planet, estimated to be over 3000 million years old. It is situated in Kappel district in the state of Karnataka and is a part of UNESCO's World Heritage Site.

Anegundi - the ancient Kishkindha - is the only setting where so many ancient sites, such as Matanga Hill, Hemakuta Hill, Malyavanta Hill, Sugreeva Cave, Rishi Mukha Hill, Tungabhadra River, Pampa Sarovar, and Bali Mountain, which are mentioned in The Ramayana, are still visible. Also, Anegundi is the only place described in The Ramayana where one chapter - Kishkindha Kanda - finishes and another chapter - Sunder Kanda - begins. Sunder Kanda is the only chapter in the epic poem where Lord Hanuman is the hero, not Lord Rama. It deals mainly with Hanuman's plight to Lanka where he proved his might, devotion, and loyalty to his masters. It is quite usual for Hindu families to chant Sundra Kanda for good omens on their auspicious occasions such as weddings, anniversaries, and birthdays.

Anegundi, a renowned pilgrim destination, was stunningly rich in archaeological and historical remains of ancient splendours and mythological surroundings. Although visitors are drawn back time and again to explore this unique combination, it is not on conventional routes and the zone is not well known to north Indian tourists. I was the most eager to see this sector as I always wanted to commence my mythical journeys and writing from this Godly place, but as they say, "Samay se Pahle aur kismet se Zaida Kabhi Nahi milta" – You get only when the time is ripe and what is written in your destiny.

ANEGUNDI HILL - HANUMAN TEMPLE

Next day, I decided to pay obeisance to Lord Hanuman and relish the sunrise from the Anegundi Hill. Most of the tourists and pilgrims take an easy option of crossing the Tungabhadra River by coracle boat. I decided to explore the route via Hospet, which did not involve a journey by boat. Also, I decided against hiring a guide so that I could move at my own pace and explore it the way I wanted.

At 5 am sharp, Tripta and I leapt into the taxi. After a few kilometres on the road, dawn mist shrouded the open area, and the lack of signposts made the journey perplexing. At every crossroad, the driver had to find someone to ask or take a guess to follow the right road as he had missed the main route. If that wasn't enough, some people were haphazardly defecating on the edges of the narrow road and would not move even when the headlights shone all over them. They shyly covered their faces with scarves and moved the water bottle slightly but kept doing their business. I thought I had made a mistake by taking this route, but the thrill of witnessing the birthplace of Hanuman kept my energy level quite high. Tripta was catching up on her sleep in the back seat. Eventually, the driver cleverly steered away and found the main road to proceed to our destination well in time.

There were many temporary hut-cum-shops at the base of the hill, but only one was open. A lady in a shabby sari was brushing the dusty floor with a worn-out broom. A few dogs were barking at each other and playing in the pleasant morning; this might have been their morning exercise. A cow was standing beside the huts while her calf was still dozing on the floor. A solitary lethargic monkey was sitting on a boulder. Perhaps he was waiting for his troops to arrive for their daily activities. It was good to see the animals in their natural state. A small carving of Anjaneri, the mother of Hanuman, greeted us from the entrance gate at the base of the hill.

It is believed that Anjaneri meditated on this hill to appeal to Lord Shiva for a son. He was so pleased with her dedication that Lord Shiva himself reincarnated as her son – Hanuman. Another school of thought believes that Hanuman was born in Anjaneri village near Nashik. Some scholars dispute this and think that his birthplace was near Gumla, in the tribal hills of Jharkhand.

Again, the weather was in our favour despite being unsettled overnight. Hanuman's white-washed temple at the top of the hill made it look as if the Parvat wore a crown on its head. We began to climb the 80-metre-high hill very cautiously as we were likely to bump into some monkeys on the way. Surprisingly, the stone steps were well-maintained. They were wide and clean, and the flight of 600 steps was appropriately lit. Although we were the only devotees climbing in the dark morning, I didn't have any kind of fear in my mind. Tripta was ahead of me as I was busy taking some snaps of the pre-twilight dawn. Soon after, a young man who appeared to be from a South Asian country took us over with big strides and was a long way ahead of us. Some glossy eyes moving left to right in the dark almost scared me to death. There were a couple of monkeys sitting between the rocks, probably having an early breakfast. I took a deep breath and moved swiftly to avoid any encounter. I prayed in my heart while carefully treading the steps to the summit.

The moment I put my foot on the terrace of the hill, I felt as fresh as the morning breeze. There was a profound stillness all around. A rhythmic humming of the Hanuman Chalisa gave me a spiritual thrill. The vista of rock mounds in the dawn light added an extra element of awe. There were astonishing far-reaching views of its low-lying surroundings in the dusky morning.

The glow of the sun began to shine on the copper-coloured soaring peaks of the boulders. On the terrace of the summit, around 20 people, presumably some priests and their disciples residing on the pinnacle, were getting ready for their yoga session as they were spreading their yoga mats. The ambience of the place was deeply spiritual. The dusky palette in the sky was turning into a greyish amber in the morning light.

A cluster of basil plants was grown in a cemented square pot on a tall platform in front of the main temple. As I entered the small temple enclave, a view of a Sandoori (orangey) coloured statue of Hanuman in the wall injected more vigour. I bowed to the Lord with folded hands. A priest in his teens, probably a disciple, rolled up his thick cotton rug and helped me to pray. He gave some offerings. I wasn't allowed to take any photos of this part of the temple.

Some soothing verses from Sunder Kanda lured me to the adjacent temple. The statues of Rama, Sita, and Lakshmana in golden yellow attire were enshrined on a small platform. A priest was doing Shingar (adornment) of the idols while another 2 were tidying up the surrounding area. One of the priests told me that the prayers related to the Lord were a 24-hour continuous process. Just opposite, in the temple hall was a rare shrine; an infant Hanuman was sitting on his mother Anjaneri's lap. These milk-white marble statues looked so cute and adorable that I stood there for a good while and cherished the atmosphere.

There were some enthusiasts already waiting for the sun to show its face. They were probably unaware of the sanctity of Hanuman's birthplace. One young lady, sitting on a dwarf rock, was shaking her legs aimlessly in the direction of the temple. I told her about it and asked her politely to show respect to the deities. She not only complied but inquired about the place as she thought it was just another hill to appreciate the sunrise. The young lady and her companion were from Brighton (UK). It gave me extra pleasure to meet someone from the same country. What a coincidence, I thought!

It felt as though we had the entire summit to ourselves. We leisurely strolled on the terrace under the open skies. The shimmering boulders with the golden streaks that stretched as far as the eye could see were uniquely awe-inspiring. I loved the tranquillity and the morning breeze buffeting my face. It was arguably the most picture-perfect spot in the whole Kishkindha area, especially in the early hours.

I sat back on the slope of the large rock near the dwelling huts of the priests and admired the enthusiasm of the young men doing their yoga asanas (postures). There was pin-drop silence, yet it was very entertaining. Like other visitors, I was encouraged to join them in yoga asanas, but I was too lazy to follow them. Perhaps there was no elasticity left in the body after the morning trek!

The sun slowly rose and brightened the horizon. For a moment in the golden light, I shut my eyes, bowed to the Sun God, and thanked Lord Hanuman for providing me with the opportunity to be so blessed. Usually, it is a lifetime's wish for Hindus to pay obeisance in such places.

The sun began to show its strength, yet it was still a pleasant downward journey. I passed many devotees in small groups hailing and praising in the name of Hanuman. Pilgrims often sang religious songs to get energy to climb up the hill. An elderly couple was resting while their family kept moving ahead. They wanted to accomplish their pilgrimage before the stone steps got hotter from the increasingly strong rays of the sun. Nevertheless, what seemed hectic in the early morning finished on a high note!!!

SHABRI ASHRAM, RISHYAMUK PARVAT AND CHINTAMANI

After a heavy and healthy breakfast, I was all set for the long day ahead. I was quite thrilled as I was going to witness some authentic sites in the footsteps of The Ramayana. Shabri Ashram was the first stop.

When Jatayu, a vulture, saw Ravana abducting Sita, he tried to rescue her from his clutches. Jatayu fought valiantly, but Ravana was too strong for him. When Rama and Lakshmana saw the dying Jatayu in their search for Sita, he told them that Ravana had gone south. En route, Rama and Lakshmana met Kabandha who was a Gandharva - a celestial musician - named Vishwa Basu. He appeared to be an ugly and carnivorous demon; he was cursed by Lord Indra. After an encounter, upon his death, Kabandha resumed his Gandharva form and directed Rama to the Rishyamuk Mountain where the exiled monkey-chief Sugreeva was hiding. Kabandha advised them to form an alliance with Sugreeva, who would be of assistance in the search for Sita. He also requested the duo to visit Shabari who was waiting to meet her Lord.

Our driver dropped us off near the jetty on the Tungabhadra River to cross over to Anegundi by either coracle or motorboat. The first impression of the riverside was uplifting. The river was gently flowing in the huge open area. It was dotted with small shiny rocks and wild bushes; some paddy fields were full of water on the west bank of the river. The whole area was surrounded by lush green trees and tall hills of boulders in the background. I am not good at poetry, but the atmosphere was surely one to inspire it.

A flight of stone-cut wide steps looked part of the scenery. I took my time to reach near the bank of the river. I spotted a local man sitting on a grey rock in the middle of the river. He was in a world of his own while meddling with his fishing gear. I mischievously shouted and asked about his well-being as if I knew him. He half-heartedly waved his hand while fiddling with a cigarette. The fishing rod next to his knee slid in the shallow waters. I cunningly looked away.

A permanent stone structure with the support of rocky pillars was set up on the bank of the river; it was used as a jetty. It looked fabulous but unsafe; there were no support barriers or any other kind of protection for the passengers, especially children and the elderly.

This was the first time that I had seen a coracle. It is a unique boat about 6 feet in diameter, shaped like an inverted bowl. It is made largely of bamboo canes and has a fine coating of bitumen on coir-sheets to make it waterproof. It moves quite fast in a spinning motion. It looked unsafe, yet they have been plied for many years. It is believed that they were the same 5 centuries ago as they are now. People do not hesitate to transport motorbikes or even sheep across the river in them.

Coracles and motorboats were the main, if not the only, modes of transport to go across to Anegundi from Hampi. The motorised boats replaced coracles between 9am and 5pm. My sense of adventure, or rather the lack of it, meant that the coracle crossing was not on my agenda; my legs were shaking at the very thought of sitting in a shaky bamboo basket as I am a bit of an aquaphobic. The coracle boats were generally filled to the brim with not just passengers but also with their accessories, such as sacks of fresh produce.

A full load of passengers in the motorboat was approaching fast in the calmly flowing river. It took longer to unload the passengers than the duration of the journey. There were more foreigners on board than Indian people.

We went across the land where the stage for the Kishkindha Kanda was all set. We passed a wooden kiosk on the left and walked along the dusty path towards the small concrete shops. A few monkeys dashed out from a small alleyway to mischievously snatch a plastic bag of bananas. This welcome made it clear that we were in Kishkindha.

It was 10 am, the mercury was rising, and the sun was glaring in my watery eyes. I took shelter under the trees on the roadside. This was the only mythical site where I came across so many foreigners in one place. They appeared to be cherishing the elegance of the natural vistas that were plentiful and wondrous. Initially, I had thought that Anegundi was not on the map for European visitors but, how wrong I was, they outnumbered the Indian tourists. When I spoke to a small group of travellers from Israel, I was amazed by their knowledge of mythological history. Some hippies with no sense of decorum for the place were busily enjoying their chillums (clay pipes), yet it was peaceful.

I expected many auto-rickshaws waiting for the pilgrims to arrive, but there was only one parked nearby. As the driver saw a few of us limping, he came up and quoted an exorbitant fare for a trip around the important sites. We didn't have an alternative, so, 4 of us had to scramble in the back, and the driver accommodated me in part of the front. I pressed my legs together and pinned my right arm to my side. There was a steel rod which I held tightly with my left hand to protect myself from slipping off the seat. A raised bolt was rubbing against my bottom. All my companions sitting in the back seat were dissolving into fits of giggles, but believe me, it was not funny at all.

After a few twists and turns on a very short, bumpy ride, he pulled over in the open area beside the shops where many drivers with their autos were waiting for their turn. The driver asked us to sit in a different auto. He told his fellow driver in his local dialect to collect the fare which he had settled with us. It seemed the auto-drivers sent only one auto-

rickshaw at a time to the disembarking area so that they could charge the maximum fare. Anyhow, the new driver was prepared to take us to some more sites for the same fare. He must have felt guilty or ashamed of charging such excessive rates.

After a few yards, the road was smooth and baked dry. The tuk-tuk seemed to go faster as we passed many paddy fields and banana groves amid landscapes laced with hills of boulders on both sides of the road. The inaccessible rocks looked golden in the sunshine and grey in the shadows. I was swept away by the impressive beauty that nature had formed by perching boulders on top of each other.

SHABRI ASHRAM

I was almost delirious with happiness as we turned right from the main road towards Shabri Dham. It was the first authentic site related to The Ramayana in Kishkindha that I was going to witness. As we entered the Pampa Sarovar and Shabri's Dham precinct, an old lady wearing multi-coloured attire and all kinds of jewellery from neck to toe, sitting under a Banyan tree cheerfully greeted us. She asked me to buy some fruit as she had a large cane basket full of red grapes and local green produce. I promised her that I would buy them later.

It didn't seem to be a place that was wrecked by decay. From a pilgrim's point of view, it was fabulous. I was taken aback by the multilayered density of Kishkindha's mythology. I bowed to Lord Ganesha, who was painted in fluorescent vermillion colour under the mango tree before climbing to the main structure. I found myself in a land of a melange of mythical, religious, and historical surroundings. The long, white-washed building tucked away in the secluded boulder hills held a mystical appeal. There was a functional temple straight ahead where a Lingam of Shiva and an image of his consort Parvati (Pampa Devi) were enshrined. It was much older than many temples in Hampi. It is believed that Goddess Pampa meditated here but married Shiva at the place where the Virupaksha temple stands today.

Pampa Sarovar and Shabri Ashram were the 2 prominent features of the precinct. Pampa Sarovar was a large rectangular pond situated right in front of the Pampa temple where the Goddess performed penance to prove her devotion to Shiva. It was surrounded by the Rocky Mountains on 3 sides. Pampa Sarovar is one of the 5 sacred Serovars; others being Manas Sarovar in Tibet, Pushkar Sarovar in Rajasthan, Bindu Sarovar in Gujarat, and Naryan Sarovar also in Gujarat where the Saraswati River ended, and the lake was filled with its water. The water in Pampa Sarovar looked murky and a little uncared for but was clean enough to do rituals such as washing your face.

Further on the far left, I spotted 2 adjacent caves that are mentioned in The Ramayana. One, where Shabri lived and prayed faithfully every day to meet Lord Rama and waited for his arrival, and the other where Rama accepted and tasted the fruits. It was the place from where Shabri directed Rama and Lakshmana to seek the help of Sugreeva and Hanuman, who lived further south, for their quest to find the whereabouts of Sita.

Fables have it that Shabri belonged to the Nishad tribal community. The night before her marriage, she saw that dozens of goats and sheep were being brought by her father to be sacrificed for the marriage dinner. Shabri was moved by this act of compassion and, fearing the cruelty to the animals, left home before the day dawned. She renounced the world and wandered around to find solace in religious places. After days of travelling, Shabri met a sage named Matanga at the base of the mountain, Rishyamuk. She became his disciple. Many years went by, and her devotion brought Shabri the ultimate reward.

When Sage Matanga was on his deathbed, he called Shabri and said, "O devotee of Rama, your austerities and devotion will not go in vain. You must wait here. Rama is sure to visit this ashram. I can say this based on my spiritual power."

Years of waiting turned Shabri into an old woman. She used to keep the place very clean and tidy for her Lord to arrive. Every day she would go out, pluck some berries and taste them to test if they were sweet or sour. If any of them was sweet, she would put it in her basket. The thought never crossed her mind that she shouldn't taste them before they were offered to the master.

Finally, at last, Lord Rama arrived at the ashram. On seeing him, Shabri's pleasure knew no bounds.

She fell at Rama's feet and said, "O Lord, I cannot describe your kindness in words. I don't have anything to offer other than my heart, but I do have some berries."

Shabri washed the holy feet and offered him the berries which she had collected from the forest that morning. The relation between the devotee and her Lord was conspicuous. Rama ate the same fruit that was tasted by Shabri.

Then Shabri inquired about the purpose of their relentless journey. Rama recounted the sad story of the kidnapping of Sita. Reflecting upon the facts, Shabri directed them to go further southwards where the monkey King, Sugreeva, lived.

I was impressed by the sheer simplicity of the caves where Shabri spent her later years. Some white-washed remnants of ancient pillars were well-preserved, showing traces of their origins. The footmarks of Lord Rama were imprinted in the stone where Shabri seated him and washed his feet. It was nicely decorated with marigold and red-orange vermillion.

A few monkeys came unannounced from the temple roof. I kept an eye on their movements. A couple of them jumped onto a mango tree. One of them was staring at me with wide red eyes. I had some nuts on me and threw them all down at once to ward off an attack.

As promised, I bought some grapes from the woman in the colourful outfit sitting under the tree. I gave her some extra money. She smiled, and in return, she gave me another bunch of grapes. As advised by Shabri, we proceeded towards the most important mission: the climb to the Rishyamuk Parvat.

RISHYAMUK PARVAT

In less than 10 minutes' drive, we were at the base of Rishyamuk Parvat, but there was no huge mountain in sight. Tripta and Indu wanted to soothe their weary legs. There was no better place than under the cluster of trees.

But Ashok wanted to accompany me. As I gazed around, it seemed the dusty grass track dropped down to the river and then rose up after the temporary crossing over the water channel towards the bushy hill. I still couldn't see any sign of the mountain that I had visualised. The driver kept pointing straight at the hill encircled by a few green trees. He guided us to cross the stream. It was the River Tungabhadra, looking sluggish.

I could not see any proper crossings to the place. Therefore, we moved further towards the shortest width of the river. The water was sparkling in the rays of the sun, and the breeze was blowing in from the vast open area. There were some cement pillars randomly lying over the flowing water channels. It appeared to be the only bridging path over the shallow waters. There was no noise apart from the smooth lapping of the waves. As I was focusing on where to place my foot appropriately on the scattered narrow pillars, a fish popped up out of the water and immediately disappeared in a gentle fizz of waves. I screamed a bit and almost stumbled. My heart rose up in my throat but somehow, I didn't fall, and crossed the wobbly bit without any jolts, but my senses had been shaken. I immediately realised that the principle of 'Karma' didn't take long to execute its doctrine, as this morning I had distracted an innocent guy sitting on the rock earning his square meal by fishing in the same river. A fish had awakened my consciousness.

The climb to Rishyamuk hill seemed easy enough to negotiate, but there was no proper path in sight. I was heading for nowhere. A dusty and green broken track ceased to exist before it even became a trail. This unspoilt green area with loose dust was the only way to penetrate the hill. Due to the soil erosion on the slope, halfway up the hill, a skeleton of a felled tree with a massive root facing upwards added to the mysterious air of the route. I didn't see any snakes, but holes pointed to their presence. We were the only visitors around. I didn't know if we were heading to the right place as the hill was interlaced with the green woods. It was not a gruelling climb, nor was it picturesque, but undoubtedly, it was a most unorthodox mountain. Still, it helped me to burn off some of the calories that I had consumed that morning.

As I put my foot on the summit, a rare glimpse of topography greeted us. A serene cement gateway surrounded by trees looked fabulous. An expanse of greenery surrounded the patches of scrub on the ridges, the small rocks that clung to the steep slopes of the hill. There were many trees such as Neem, Peepal, keekar, and Bargadh that added to the beauty of this exceptional hill.

The tranquillity was unique. There was no sound apart from an occasional rustling of the leaves. It took a while for my ears to adjust to the sudden shift in volume, or lack of it. The true silence confirmed that it was the Rishyamuk Parvat, the Mook hill where rishis performed their penance. It felt as if I had landed in the era of The Ramayana.

I moved ahead towards the terrace where a holy man, in a cotton dhoti and kurta, along with another person, was sitting on a small platform under the tinned roof on the right near the cave. Some elaborate murals of Lord Rama, Lakshmana, and Hanuman on the back wall made it look very colourful. I roamed around the huge courtyard in front of the cave temple. It was so tranquil that I let myself sink into the surroundings. The reality of the scene was a close match to its description in religious books and even to what I had seen in television serials. I took a breather and more photos.

The holy man kept looking at us. I went to him and said, "I have never witnessed such a moment of stillness in my life. My senses are getting rejuvenated by the sight of the landscapes and the natural soundtrack."

He welcomed us with a smile and asked about our whereabouts. I squatted next to him on the clean, thin rug and said, "Pundit ji, I thought this mountain would be very tall and isolated, but it is tucked away amongst boulders."

He began to unfold the mythology and further layers of historic marvels. He turned his face towards me and said, "Though everything is threatened by pollution and climate change, this place is still unspoilt. If you roam around the summit and feel the silence, you could imagine that this place was created in the heavens and lowered down to Earth. Therefore, you are in the land of Gods."

During his talk of the sight, he recited a few verses. He was melodic in his approach to The Ramayana. Although I have heard the mythology so many times, it was still fascinating to hear it again from the priest who manned the place where the principal incidents took place. It felt as if I had made a pilgrimage, although this was never intended.

The Rishyamuk Parvat was the most significant hill in many ways. First, Sugreeva and Hanuman, along with their forces, lived here. Sugreeva hid away from his mighty brother, Bali, who could not attack here due to the curse incurred upon him. Second and foremost, Hanuman met Rama and Lakshmana for the first time.

It is believed that when Rama and Lakshmana reached near the base of the hill, Sugreeva's spies saw 2 men in saintly dress armed with bows and arrows. They rushed to the King and expressed their suspicion. Worried, Sugreeva immediately sent Hanuman to verify the news as he thought his brother, Bali, might have sent them to spy on his kingdom. Hanuman disguised himself as a Brahmin and went to meet the princes. On finding out their identity, Hanuman reverted to his real form and bowed to them. Hanuman gladly carried them on his shoulders to the top of the mountain. After Rama related the story of their exile and Sita's abduction, Sugreeva promised them that he would accomplish the task of rescuing Sita. He requested Rama to help him fight against the oppression of Bali who had taken away his wife, Tara, and the kingdom. Rama readily agreed.

I was very keen to see the solitary temple in India where Lord Hanuman and Sugreeva were enshrined together. The priest got up with the help of crutches as half of his leg had been amputated. He looked very excited to show us around. I eagerly followed him to the narrow cave which became a tiny temple after a few feet. The cave was high and wide enough to pass comfortably though a slight leak of water was conspicuous. It was probably the condensation dripping off the ceiling. The temple was a cave dug in the boulders and retained its glory and mystery. The holy man gave us some offerings and blessed us by sprinkling holy water.

When I asked the priest about the boulder-strewn hills all around, he smiled and said, "Every inch of the place is soaked in mythology and history. If you scratch the surface anywhere around this area, you will uncover and feel the authenticity of Kishkindha. You might visit the prominent places here, yet you would barely touch the sites of Anegundi that were once a part of Kishkindha. Many of them are inaccessible now. So, if you think Ramayana is a myth, think again."

At the base of the hill, calm flowing water was bordered by land where a herd of cows was grazing in the middle, unaware of the importance of the place. I would have preferred more time to admire the tranquillity before being whisked off to the next site, but the clock was ticking fast.

CHINTAMANI

My next stop was a short drive away. As we turned towards the Chintamani cave and temple, there were narrow streets lined with old brick houses. It was hard to spot without the help of a guide or a local. When we reached the end of the residential streets, we entered an open area where views of the river and rock-strewn hills in every direction greeted us.

The Chintamani temple on the right was hard to miss. We strolled up to the white-washed structure in the cloudless heat. Lord Shiva's Lingam was enshrined in a small but clean temple.

An old woman in a faded printed sari followed us as soon as we entered the Chintamani area. She tried to narrate the significance of every site by walking ahead of us. She sounded quite knowledgeable. The seventy-plus enthusiast was walking barefoot with the help of a bamboo stick. I called her Amma (Mother) and took her as my guide.

She began to explain the history and mythology while walking towards the Chintamani cave. "This is the last visited cave; barely a handful of visitors venture out into this corner, hence unmanned. Sugreeva promised to help Rama in locating the whereabouts of Sita. Along with Hanuman, they planned a strategy to kill Bali on this hill."

It was very quiet and pleasant with not too many tourists. We were in an open expanse where the remains of mythology were still evident. A sound of steady whacking caught my attention. I gazed in wonder; my eyes scanned the breathtaking landscape. Many ladies were thwacking their washing on the riverbank near the solitary stone structure, while the young children spread the colourful clothes on the flat rocks to dry. Some cows were grazing in the hedges below the hills across the river. The scene helped me understand the rural lives of the local people. I shifted my gaze and followed Amma.

Amma began to tell the mythical stories and her face lit up like that of a child. She was a non-stop narrator. Despite having a bad knee, her excitement enabled her to keep up a fast pace. She took us to the cave where the planning was carried out. This peculiar place was tucked away in the secluded hill. Naturally formed boulders, which supported and perched on each other, looked like a few caves in the vicinity.

Understandably, there was a pin-drop silence; it was an eerie sight. The flat stone in the middle is believed to be the seat where Lord Rama sat during the planning. A small stone with engravings of Rama and Lakshmana was placed to make it look like a shrine. Amma told me that since Lord Rama gave a Chintamani - a precious stone - to identify Hanuman as his messenger to Sita. The place was called Chintamani.

As we came out of the cave, there was an impression of footprints of Rama on a raised rocky sheet facing Bali Parvat across the river. It is believed to be the spot where Rama stood and shot an arrow. There were supposed to be 7 Sol trees in front of the target, but Rama's arrow pierced all of them and hit Bali. Just in front of the footprints, there was an impression of a bow and arrows on the flat rock so that the pilgrims could envisage the history.

Apparently, Lord Rama suggested Sugreeva have a duel with his half-brother Bali, and Rama would shoot him down. As planned, when the duel was in progress, Sugreeva waited for the ultimate result, but Rama couldn't differentiate one from another as they looked identical. The next day, Rama suggested that Sugreeva should wear a garland of marigolds around his neck. Consequently, when they were engaged in a fight again, Rama shot an arrow at Bali's back.

There was a rock shelter where Rama stayed for a few days following the event. Amma showed us some of the less visited sites. She ran up the steep hill like a goat. I wanted to stroll around some boulders but didn't venture to climb them because of the threat from falling rocks; the buzzing of insects deterred me too.

I held Amma's soft hands between my palms and appreciated her guidance. I gave her remuneration 3 times more than she expected, though it was a meagre amount in Sterling; the glow on her face was priceless and timeless. She hugged me tightly. I could see my grandmother in her.

After walking all morning, it sharpened my appetite. We took a break for a quick lunch. As usual, I ate more than my usual quota; therefore, an afternoon siesta was justified.

MALYAWANTA HILL

Whenever I left the hotel, the adventure was rarely far away. The next morning, Malyawanta Hill was the prime site on my list. After visiting the museum in Kamlapur, we headed to one of the highest hills in the region. Malyawanta Hill was detached from the rest of the tourist circuit, and many visitors often fail to make it to this beautiful place. I was told that I could salute the sun in the morning and wave it goodbye in the evening. Unfortunately, I could not fit in these events.

This hill has great significance in terms of mythology and history. First and foremost, Rama spent most of his time on this Parvat during his stay in Kishkindha. This was the place from where he really began his search for Sita. Hanumana conveyed the good news of locating her whereabouts in Lanka at this very place. Strategically, this hill was very useful because Rama could keep an eye on all directions from its high altitude.

As we passed huge boulders at the base of the hill, a cement gate to the Malyawanta Hill attracted my attention. Some massive rocks had tumbled down the hillside. This Parvat was one of the few hilltops in the region where the vehicle could be taken right up to the temple complex.

Rama released an arrow towards the Malyawanta Parvat. It created a cleft on the boulder at the top of the hill, and he decided to live there until the monsoon was over.

I came out of the car and gazed around, 'mind-blowing,' I mumbled to myself. The anonymous ancient monuments and some ruined sites that were scattered all around gave the feel that a gigantic map of Hampi and Kishkindha still existed side by side. Some patches of green paddy dotted with palm trees and brown boulders precariously stretching into the horizon looked like a completed jigsaw puzzle. The slow-moving water of the Tungabhadra River was like a huge snake slithering between them. It was an exhilarating sight.

We went through the towered porch into the temple complex where there were a few temples and a pavilion adorning the hill-top. On the left, it seemed as if a long chain of boulder mounds had made a golden-brown garland.

The Malyawanta Raghunatha temple was the most significant site. It is dedicated to Lord Rama. This was the temple where Rama gave the Chura-mani to Hanumana as a token to show Sita. The inner shrine housed the images of Rama and Lakshmana who are sitting; Hanumana is kneeling and does not have his Gadha in his hand. This is the only temple in India where Rama is depicted in the meditating posture, with no bow and arrow in his hand. It might be representing the sorrow he felt when missing his consort.

A white-washed shrine towered over a gigantic boulder, the highlight of the summit. It could be seen from any angle. A Lingam of Shiva was housed beneath the boulder. An array of carved statues of Nandi graced the front of the shrine.

Although it was in an isolated site, it was easy to explore the important place where Lord Rama spent 4 months of his exile. The soulful calmness and the mythological sites kept me on the Parvat longer than I intended.

I was glad that I had the stamina to walk around most of the day. But I was tired by the evening and somehow managed to eat a little and make my way back to the hotel room. Within a few minutes, I was asleep for the rest of the night.

On the last day, I was sad but ready to return with amazing photographs and treasured memories of a richly illustrated past.

RAMESHWARAM AND DHANUSH KODI

We could have made an early morning journey in a taxi from Kanyakumari, the southernmost town of India, to Rameshwaram. Instead, we chose a night train to give us an extra day to explore the grandeur of the temples around the area. It was ideal for a group of 8 friends: Janak and I, 2 couples from England, and one from Navi Mumbai.

After an overnight journey, when the train halted on the tracks, many guides and porters began to harass us. They kept chasing and asking if we needed their services in the temples or for accommodation purposes. We ignored them all and hired a taxi to the main bazaar where the hotels were plentiful. We couldn't find a comfortable hotel as most of them provided basic facilities, running water, so-called showers, some having western toilets and air conditioners but never working to their full capacity. Eventually, we chose the best one in the market area. Typically, our room had a distinctive smell of damp that became negligible after a while; either it evaporated with the opening of the doors, or the air-conditioner did its job. More than likely, we just got accustomed to it. We were in the land that every Hindu would like to visit before he dies.

Rameshwaram is an island situated in the Gulf of Mannar at the southern tip of the Indian peninsula, connected by one of India's engineering wonders, the Indira Gandhi Bridge. It is a bustling small village town attracting hordes of devotees and tourists alike due to its immense religious and geographical significance. According to the Vedas and Puranas, this is the place where Rama worshipped Lord Shiva to cleanse away the sins of killing a Brahmin, Ravana. The entire area is associated with the numerous incidents that took place during The Ramayana era.

The Ramanathaswami temple is the most notable historical shrine on the island. The primary deity of the temple is Shiva in the form of a Lingam. The whole temple premises are home to many shrines; it has huge gateway towers in every direction. The main temple is encircled by high walls on all sides. In its interiors, there are striking long corridors. One of them is lavishly designed and stunning. It is around 200 metres long, 6 metres wide, and over 9 metres high. Its 1212 gigantic pillars rest on a 1.5-metre-high platform, and its symmetrical arches with lion heads on both sides draw attention from every angle. Sculptures transformed every column, lint, and arch into a work of art. Each pillar was skilfully carved with individual compositions; their granite shafts were decorated with scrollwork and lotus motifs, enhancing the beauty of the corridor. The contribution of the Jaffna kings of the Sethupathy dynasty to the temple was considerable; many stone blocks were shipped from Koneshwaram temple in Trincomalee (Sri Lanka) to this temple to renovate its sanctum sanctorum.

As we were still being pestered by the usual priests and guides, I consulted the manager of the hotel and made a wise decision to hire a priest-cum-guide for the whole morning. Our priest, A. Rajendran, advised us to visit the temple immediately to beat the crowds as there weren't many pilgrims in the vicinity at this time.

I was very excited in my heart as bathing in holy water is a major and rare event of the pilgrimage to Rameshwaram. Mr Rajendran explained everything patiently. He outlined all the ceremonies of the morning and told us how to perform the rituals in the temple. He suggested that we should wear some casual outfits while performing the rituals of pouring water over our heads from 22 Tirthas - holy water-wells. There were 37 wells in the vicinity, but 15 are defunct.

In line with the rituals, we were to have a dip in the Agni-tirtha before praying in the main shrine. Hence, we followed our priest to the Agni-tirtha on the sea; it was around 210 metres to the east of the temple. The tiled path leading to the sea looked bare compared to the area around the temple. It is believed to be the place where Lord Rama worshipped Lord Shiva and bathed in the sea to absolve himself from killing Ravana.

This Tirtha was a shallow sea where pilgrims were taking a dip in the warm water. I was ready to comply with our guide's instructions, but Janak was hesitant to step into the sea due to its surroundings. Some pieces of dirty cloth were scattered all around the floor; the water looked murky, and garbage could be seen on the steps. I held Janak's hand tightly and said, "What the heck, let's go in and have a dip! The holy water of 22 wells will be poured over our heads, and that will wash away all the dirt." She smiled and nodded in agreement.

We slowly waded into the water and went deeper to avoid the crowd; the water looked cleaner there. As I splashed some water on her face and pulled her further, she quickly dipped her head as she sensed my mischievous intentions. Anyhow, we followed our priest to perform the next ceremony of pouring water over the head from the wells.

On the way back to the Ramanathaswami temple, we were halted by a herd of dozy cows in the middle of the road, probably looking for some fodder. With some turns and twists, we kept following our priest who was carrying a small bucket in his hand; a long thin rope was tied to the arched handle of the bucket to fetch some water from the wells. As the temple began to get busier, Rajendran decided to take us through the VIP route; it was a hassle-free path, but we had to pay some extra money for the privileged service. When he took us through some 'no entry' passages towards the holy wells, I looked at him curiously. He said with a smile, "The temple authorities have plans to renovate and widen the pathways to the holy wells." Anyhow, it suited us to the hilt. There were many pilgrims wandering around the wells, but only a few of them had hired guides. Some people had no idea about the rituals and looked lost.

Rajendran started his job perfectly well in accordance with the rituals. He drew some water from the well, poured it over our heads, and rushed to the next well to repeat the same routine. Each well was fenced with a half-metre tall brick wall; many of these wells were next to each other. The brick floor looked very clean, considering so much water being splashed all around. Rajendran was quick enough to fetch the water out of the well and splash it on everyone's head, yet steady enough to let everyone enjoy the ambience. He was sharp to throw the brass bucket like a stone into the well, yet faster to pull the rope with long stretchy arms. He mentioned that there is a difference in the taste of water in each well. I tried a few sips randomly but couldn't differentiate from one to another.

Fourteen out of 22 wells were inside the temple area, and the rest were outside the zone but still in the temple vicinity. Anyhow, Rajendran took us to the outer zone and explained the importance of each well. Every time the priest poured the water on my head, he said with a smirk, "Do you want to try it again to taste and experience it for yourself?" I replied in the negative. It was soothing physically and spiritually when he was pouring the holy water; maybe I was really concentrating to do everything in accordance with the rituals. It is believed that a bath in all the wells is considered the ultimate parihara - a remedial measure - for all sins as well as having curative properties. The priest accomplished his task with great vigour, and the whole bathing process took less than an hour.

He hung the bucket on his shoulder, wiped the sweat from his forehead with a red striped cotton scarf, and asked, "How do you feel spiritually?"

It was hard to explain, but I said to him, "I feel elated and lucky to have accomplished these rituals in a traditional manner. I am delighted to find out many historical and mythical facts."

We finished our brunch just before noon and returned to the temple. There were still lots of pilgrims gathered around the main gate of the temple to pay their obeisance.

I asked our guide, "Is it a special day today?"

He said, while sorting out some necessary puja items from his shoulder bag, "It isn't unusual to see a flood of pilgrims; the temple is crowded all year round and becomes very busy during the festive season, especially on Shivaratri - Shiva's birthday and Rama Navami - Rama's birthday."

The priest took us to the main gate of the temple and narrated the history of the temple in great depth. According to Puranas - ancient texts, Rama had fixed an auspicious time for the puja of the Lingam. He sent Hanumana to Mount Kailasha to bring a Vishwalingam - a sacred Shiva stone established for worship by Hindus across the world. As Hanumana was a staunch devotee of Shiva, he began to worship his Lord on the mountain, thus he couldn't return in time for the ceremony. Consequently, Sita created a Lingam out of the sand to perform the pooja. When Hanumana returned with the Vishwalingam, the necessary ceremony was over. Hanumana was annoyed and with the permission of Lord Rama, he attempted to remove the sand Lingam with the aid of his tail, but when he was unable to do so, he realised the divinity of Sita and bowed to her. To comfort the disappointed Hanumana, Lord Rama told him to install the Vishvalingam on the north side of the temple near the main gate and declared that devotees must worship it before the Ramanathan Lingam.

Immediately, we proceeded to the platform where Mr Rajendran performed a puja of the offerings that we were going to present before the main deity: the offerings consisted of some flowers, an apple, a banana, yogurt, honey, and a small canister of holy Ganges water. It took 20 minutes to conduct the initial puja; he chanted a few mantras while putting all the offerings in a small basket. We continued towards the main deities.

We had a choice of 2 routes to go to the main sanctum; one was an ordinary route for general devotees paying a nominal amount, and the second was for the devotees who could afford to pay a little more and was therefore less crowded. I felt very bad about it, but due to time constraints, we decided to follow him through a VIP queue.

"Why do you have to pay to visit a religious place and also pay a different price for a different queue?" I questioned our guide.

"It is to maintain the infrastructure of the temple and to control the flow of the pilgrims," he vaguely replied.

There were many murals of The Ramayana era on the walls all around the main sanctum, especially the incidents which took place around

Rameshwaram area: Rama, Sita, and Lakshmana conducting the puja of the Lingam; Hanuman and other vanaras and bears constructing the bridge across the sea. The main shrine looked simple but attractive; the solid wooden door covered with a silver sheet was beautifully carved. A priest came out from the inner shrine holding a thaali - a large round silver plate - of puja in his hand. He conducted an elaborate puja for us; chanting of some mantras made the atmosphere livelier. The higher-priced ticket provided us with extra time in front of the deity.

It felt very soothing sitting right in front of the principal deity. I felt as if I was sitting under the shadow of God himself and he was blessing me. There was lots of noise coming from the devotees, yet I felt calm and peaceful; even with a loud chanting of mantras, it felt restful. The Lingam and its surrounding area were beautifully decorated with flowers and gold ornaments. Lots of fruits and flowers were arranged on a platform near the back wall. Some silver and brass aarti pots filled with ghee-soaked wicks were twinkling all around the Lingam, and the fragrance of scores of incense sticks was captivating. There were 5 or 6 priests inside the shrine who were busy taking offerings from the devotees, and after touching those offerings at the feet of the deity, they returned them to the related devotee as prasad, the God's blessings. There was yet another temple to the right of the presiding deity where Shiva's consort, Parvati, was enshrined. Usually, in a Shiva temple, Parvati is found to the left of the Lord. But here, that tradition was not followed.

The ambience in the temple complex was joyous: devotees in small groups looked cheerful while sorting out their prasad and admiring the temple structure. Its corridors looked breathtakingly beautiful, so much so, my friend had to drag me off as I was engrossed in admiring the subtly lavish architecture and carvings on the pillars and the ceiling. It was an amazing display of artistic talent; I was enthralled by it. The richly carved granite pillars on the mounted platform were symmetrical; well-balanced lion heads on the pillars looked enchanting. The ceiling was artfully painted in various designs; the soft lighting enhanced its artistry. Strangely, there was no noise in the corridors despite being busy with so many devotees.

There was a vibrant atmosphere in the market around the temple vicinity; cheerful tourists wandered around the town to buy some exquisite souvenirs. A variety of ornamental items made up of palm leaves and sea shells seemed to be their first choice. The surrounding market was awash with stalls and some small shops selling conches, shell jewellery, soft toys, and various kinds of gift items. Some cows wandered through the crowds, munching on offerings of grass and marigold thrown in their way. I was ready for much-needed nourishment. As vegetarianism is still a part and parcel of daily cuisine in many pilgrimage towns, Rameshwaram was no different. There was a good choice of South Indian dishes including idlis, dosas, etc., and I chose a masala dosa. It was served with sambhar and 2 kinds of coconut chutneys. I thoroughly enjoyed the well-deserved brunch and a siesta soon after.

DHANUSHKODI

I was tossing and turning with excitement the night before I was going to visit the most striking and peculiar place, Dhanushkodi. I didn't know what to expect from this region. Although my first trip, in August 2001, to Rameshwaram was only a flying visit to the temple of Ranganatha, I had never known that Dhanush Kodi was a part of the Rameshwaram Island, or that I was so near to the place until I began to research The Ramayana trail.

The day began with the sounds of bells and devotional chanting from the temple, surely one of the most beautiful wake-up calls I experienced. I was out on the sandy beach near the Ramanathaswami temple before dawn had broken. I restlessly strolled up and down the beach watching fishermen coming back from their routine work, pulling dinghy boats, carrying their belongings, and sorting out some fishing nets and ropes, etc. The smell of fish was hanging in the air, but some staunch joggers were busy running from one end to another. As soon as it turned 6, I rushed back to the hotel to wake everybody up for an early breakfast.

Our driver-cum-guide, Krishnan, as arranged on the previous night, arrived at 7.30. He asked us to settle in the middle row and on the back seats in a Mahindra jeep which looked like it had seen better days. It was rusty and discoloured. We had no choice but to sit on the torn spongy seats as there weren't many four-wheel-drive vehicles available. We were ready for a 20-kilometre adventurous trip to Dhanushkodi, a place hardly known as a tourist destination.

After we crossed the narrow roads of Rameshwaram town and a few kilometres of densely wooded area dotted with huts on either side of the road, we were suddenly in the open air. It was picturesque beyond a huge wasteland. On the left side, the ocean looked quiet and placid like a vast mirage in the desert, but on the right, the water was roaring constantly with high waves. We drove past miles and miles of unbroken beach, without a soul in sight, along the deserted shores - the essence of true solitude.

Around an 8 km drive brought us to our first stop at Kothandaram temple, also known as the Vibhishna temple. We turned left from the main road; the temple was hidden behind the bushes on the edge of a small lake. This was the place where Vibhishna joined Rama's forces.

A legend goes that when Vibhishna asked his brother, Ravana, to return Sita to her husband, Rama, promptly and unharmed, his advice was ignored. Instead, Ravana exiled Vibhishana from Lanka. Before he left, he went to see his mother Kaikesi, who advised him to go and serve Rama, who was at the time assembling his forces to attack Ravana.

The temple was on a small sandy hillock surrounded by the ocean on all 4 sides. The lush foliage around the temple added to the beauty of the place. The bronze idols of Rama, Sita, Lakshmana, and Vibhishna were enshrined inside the temple. The walls were beautifully decorated with marvellous murals that represented the story of The Ramayana. It seemed some renovations had been done to the outer part of the building as the boundary wall looked newly plastered along the elevation of the place. The stone steps on the platform around the shrine were gracefully restored. It captured the mind and imagination of ancient India.

In the recent past, this historical temple could have been lost as the shrine was threatened by work to re-align a canal in the area. The decision was changed after lots of protests by locals whose livelihood was dependent on pilgrims coming to the temple.

"When a furious cyclone in 1964 could not harm the temple, how could mankind?" said the priest.

Back on the road, the speedometer of the old jeep seldom crossed the 30-kilometre line. It was good in a way; we enjoyed the scenery. The road to Dhanushkodi was lined with casuarina plants on either side of the road. After 6 kilometres, we abruptly reached a fishing village, Moonram Chathiram, where all forms of transport to Dhanushkodi stopped; some young officers were manning a navy post nearby. The road literally ended there. If you haven't arrived here in a four-wheel drive, you need to hire a vehicle more suitable for the sandy terrain to traverse the mud tracks leading up to the end of the land, near the confluence of 2 seas.

Our driver went out and left us in the vehicle for a while. The smell of rotting fish and garbage hung heavily in the air around the village. Some goats, hens, and stray dogs were roaming near the shanty huts that dotted the beach; thorny bushes, dirty plastic bags, and general refuse were scattered all over. We had thrown some snacks towards the animals; unsurprisingly, they started to fight as if they had not been fed for weeks.

A few four-wheel drive open-end trucks were waiting for the pilgrims who arrive here by bus or three-wheelers. They generally charge a set price for the truck, which you can share with other passengers. Sometimes they take as many passengers as they can accommodate, including many standing on the loading lid at the back.

After a few minutes, our driver came back with a hammer and some small iron discs in his hand. He put those discs somewhere in the back wheels, and consequently, the jeep became a four-wheel drive. A shabby-looking teenager, claiming to be his assistant, accompanied him with 2 pieces of rough timber in his hand. Before the journey began, the jeep jolted and stopped. Although the engine fired again without any problem, a fear arose in my mind about what would happen if it broke down in the middle of nowhere.

As I was praying to Lord Hanumana to keep everything in working order, my wife sarcastically asked the teenager, "Why are you carrying these pieces of wood? Are you making a boat or something?"

He innocently explained, "When the jeep speeds in the shallow lagoon over ankle-deep waters, it splashes all around, and at the same time, the other side of the jeep's wheels go deep in the wet sand track, made by the continuous traffic. So, sometimes the loose wet sand requires an assistant's support to place rough wooden pieces or boards under the wheels at many places for traction."

An uninterrupted, vast expanse of sand dunes ran along an endless sight of the sea. As we were passing the dry sand dunes, dust swirled around our jeep and followed us. Weaving through the dunes, the temporarily made path sometimes disappeared into the sand. The driver looked well trained to steer the jeep in these dunes. He was following the bumpy sand lanes etched out by the flow of traffic. The sand dunes were so uneven, only the driver knew where and when to steer; he must have had a navigator in his head. I nearly fell off my seat as I was right behind the driver. The others were laughing madly as they were finding it hard to hold on to their seats without armrests. Janak had a smirk on her face as she was the only one who was sitting steadily holding the side door handle. In fact, it reminded me of the journey of a Desert Safari in a 4x4 drive in Dubai where your heart fills with joy and you get a thrill out of the bumpy rides. The guffawing of Ashok and Indu was deafening, Yogesh couldn't control his laughter while Tripta was holding on to an iron rod as well as his arm, Raman and Rama were rolling deliberately onto each other on the back seat, it seemed they were getting a buzz out of every turn and twist. Squeals and giggles filled the atmosphere.

We meandered on uneven tracks along the seashore and amongst abandoned shanty huts. The sea on the left accompanied us all along the way. It seemed we were the only travellers, all alone on the lost island. At times, it was scary, but I kept my eyes on the track ahead. At one stage, it felt as if we were transported to the middle of nowhere and had been travelling for miles and miles and for hours and hours. We were rattled and jolted for nearly 25 minutes. The six-kilometre ride brought us to the actual ruins; a deserted town slowly appeared before us.

It didn't take long to comprehend that this was the ghost town - as declared by the Government of Tamil Nadu - of Dhanushkodi. The ruined buildings, an abandoned church, and remnants of a solitary temple greeted us as we halted there. It was rather a baffling set of ruins with decaying landmarks: a derelict railway station, scattered railway tracks, and the skeletal remains of boats, all narrating the poignant story of people uprooted by nature. In some places, the wild shrubs and half-drying leaves were partly covered with the sand dust. On the wet sands, an isolated plank of rotten wood covered with moss appeared to be the resting point for the birds. This small strip of island was filled with history to the brim, it kept me on my toes.

HISTORY AND THE TRAGEDY

Dhanushkodi is a small hamlet at the southern tip of Rameshwaram Island on the eastern coast of Tamil Nadu state in India. It is only 29 kilometres west of Talaimannar in Sri Lanka, one of the shortest land borders in the world. Primarily, Dhanushkodi draws pilgrims and tourists to visit the mysterious Rama Setu, also known as Adam's Bridge or Causeway. Rama Setu is made entirely of limestone and holds great religious significance for Hindus, as they believe the bridge was built by Lord Rama in his quest to reach the land of Lanka to free his wife from Ravana.

According to Hindu scriptures, after the Lanka war, when Rama returned victorious to India, Vibhishna requested Rama to break the Sethu so that no other army was able to use it. Rama broke the connecting point of the bridge on the Indian side with one end of his bow, and thus the name Dhanushkodi – Dhanush meaning bow and Kodi means the end. But why would he do that, and why would someone attack Lanka again? This remains something of a mystery. It is also believed that Rama may have marked this spot to build the Sethu with one end of his bow. This theory sounds more realistic to me.

According to history, as I have mentioned earlier, Surpnakha, the sister of Ravana, proposed to Lord Rama during his 14-year exile. When Lord Rama turned her down, in a rage, Surpnakha started to insult Sita. Lakshmana was furious with this behaviour and, in anger, he cut off her nose and ears. Ravana, in turn, abducted Sita to avenge the insult meted out to his sister. Hence, Lord Rama mobilised his force of monkeys and bears to build the bridge, which was used to cross over to Lanka and rescue Sita from Ravana.

Lord Rama prayed to the sea God for 3 days and 3 nights; to allow him and his forces to cross over to Lanka but the sea God didn't take any notice of Lord Rama's request to lower the level of water. This annoyed Lord Rama. When Rama was about to release an arrow, presented by Lord Brahma, into the water, the sea God appeared before him and requested him not to dry up the sea for the sake of the sea creatures and advised him to consult Nala, the son of Vishwakarma - an engineer of the Gods, to build the bridge. Nala obeyed the orders of Lord Rama and built a 30-kilometre-long monumental bridge in the middle of the ocean. It is claimed the crossing was a marvel of engineering. Allegedly, the bridge was passable on foot until the channel deepened in the 15th century. There are some temple records that show Rama Setu was comprehensively above sea level until it broke in 1480 CE. Valmiki has described the construction of Rama Setu in his Ramayana on the southern shore in India. This was also alluded to by Veda Vyasa in Mahabharata when he referred to the Sethu as Nala Sethu. Anyhow, why doubt the construction of Rama Setu by Rama when nobody else in world history has ever claimed its construction?

Many historians from different parts of the world have described the bridge as Ram's Setu. The maps in Schwartzberg's historical atlas show the bridge as Ram's Setu. The texts by Marco Polo call this area Sethu-bandha, meaning 'bridge on the sea.' In 1804, a British cartographer prepared a map where he called this area by the name Adam's Bridge. Even pictures from a NASA Satellite have shown the existence of a straight stretch of rocks in the Palk Strait between Dhanushkodi and Talaimannar in Sri Lanka.

Another mythological story about the construction of Rama Setu is prevalent among Hindus: Lord Rama's encounter with a squirrel.

After Nala, the engineer, was consulted about the construction of Rama Setu, Lord Rama told Sugreeva, the king of monkeys, to take charge of the whole project. Sugreeva's army, monkeys and giant bears, went all around the mountains where they uprooted trees and boulders to build the bridge. One day Lord Rama went to the construction site to see the progress of the bridge. Rama's heart filled with joy to see the army of monkeys and bears working extremely hard to complete the project. Nala went to Lord Rama to report on the work. Coincidentally, a group of monkeys and bears saw a small brown squirrel running back and forth, carrying pebbles in her mouth and placing them alongside a huge boulder. Sometimes, she would dip in the sea to wet her fur and roll in the sand. Then, immediately, she would run to the construction site and shake off all the sand from her back. The monkeys and the bears were making fun of her. Some of them even tried to catch her but she proved too quick for all of them. The squirrel dodged all the monkeys and the bears and ran straight up to Lord Rama's feet. As Nala was busy updating Rama on the project, the squirrel stood on her haunches and spoke as loud as she could. Lord Rama heard the squirrel's voice above the din and the gurgle of the sea. Lord Rama knelt, lifted the beautiful creature between his 2 palms and asked about her well-being. The squirrel's eyes filled with tears, and she explained everything about the mockery she was facing at the hands of the horrid monkeys and bears. Rama's heart melted with the squirrel's dedication. He acknowledged her contribution and said, "The Bridge will be made stronger by the pebbles and the sand you have carried and from now onwards, nobody will make fun of your physical appearance." Rama then gently stroked the squirrel on her back with his fingers. When he raised his hand, the marks of his fingers were left on the squirrel's brown fur. According to the myth, ever since the squirrel carried 3 white stripes on her back, as a token of Rama's affection. This association with Rama explains why squirrels are considered sacred in India. This reminded me of when my grandmother used to stop me from throwing stones at squirrels in my childhood.

This shore of Dhanushkodi is very peculiar: on one side are the waters of the Indian Ocean known as Ratnakaran and on the other are the waters of the Bay of Bengal known as Mahodadhi. The sandbars in a straight line, seen at a distance in the middle of these seas, are believed to be the remnants of the original Rama Setu. It is also believed that Lord Rama bathed at this juncture of 2 seas to atone for the sin of killing Ravana. Therefore, the place where the 2 seas meet is also known as Punya Tirtha - a sacred site. As this confluence is shaped like a bow, and the strip of land resembles an arrow poised for release, devout Hindus consider the Sethu in the middle of the seas to be an arrow; hence they venerate this place as very holy. They perform religious rites here too.

The government, at one stage, hired dredgers equipped with cutters to develop a channel for large ships which could have reduced the sailing time from the west coast to the east. Some groups demanded that the Rama Setu should be saved for the sake of heritage and to prevent an ecological disaster. Anyhow, the remains of Rama Setu put up stiff resistance and proved difficult to remove. Eventually, the dredgers had to retire from the scene. Devout Hindus argued it was Lord Rama's might that they couldn't eradicate. Some described these attempts to remove the Rama Setu as an effort to make it more convenient for British ships to navigate between Dhanushkodi and Talaimannar during British rule. Recently, the Science Channel used satellite imagery from NASA and other pieces of evidence to prove the existence of Rama Setu. They explain that the rocks connecting India and Sri Lanka are sitting on a sandbar, also known as the shoals, and the investigators believe that the sandbar is natural, but the stones sitting on top of it are not.

Although there was a small ferry service between the 2 sites, it was suspended in 1982 because of tensions between Sri Lankan forces and the separatists - The Liberation Tamil Tigers of Eelam - especially in northern Sri Lanka. But now, there is no fighting of any sort in Sri Lanka, hence the respective governments should take an initiative to revive the ferry service. When I glanced at the landscape of this spectacular corner of Rameshwaram Island, I couldn't think of a more deserving location for improvement. In recent years, the central government has paid more attention to the basic infrastructure, road network, and better transportation system right up to the last shore. Dhanushkodi was turned into a ghost town after a cyclone in 1964. Since then, no efforts have been made to regenerate this area.

On the fateful night of 22nd Dec 1964, the sea suddenly swelled and lashed the harbour town of Dhanushkodi with gigantic tidal waves from the Palk Straits followed by a dreadful cyclone. The whole hamlet was swept away. The railway station, post office, places of worship, houses, and all government buildings were also destroyed. After an atrocious night, a sad morning witnessed sand dunes burying the entire village, never to be inhabited again. Nearly everyone died, and every building was reduced to rubble; only a few animals survived. It was one of the worst cyclones to hit southern India in recorded history. The government of Madras - present-day Chennai - immediately declared Dhanushkodi a ghost town.

During that dreadful night, a train with over 115 passengers drowned in the sea. A large group of students from Madurai city had boarded the train to Dhanushkodi. Some students alighted at the Pamban station near Rameshwaram, and the rest carried on to Dhanushkodi. But none of them knew they were heading to their burial place. It is believed that the driver of the train had refused to move the carriage from the nearby station and informed the control office in Madurai about the weather conditions. But the then higher officials paid no heed to his repeated warnings and asked him to proceed to the next destination, Dhanushkodi. Consequently, the train was ripped from the tracks and thrown many yards away by the severe force of the tidal waves. After the disaster, the railway lines were never repaired, and sand covered the damaged tracks.

Despite its remoteness, this part of the island has a history of human occupation before the cyclone: the skeletal structures of the buildings that survived the cyclone still exist, partly buried in the sand and partly weathered by the sea, adding a mysterious and sad look to the place. Human habitation is almost non-existent; there is no permanent human settlement, only a few fishermen live with their families in thatched huts. Some of them sell water bottles, snacks, and small pieces of the stones of Adam's Bridge (coral, as souvenirs) for their survival.

Before 22-23 Dec 1964, Dhanushkodi was a flourishing tourist and pilgrimage town. Many ferries ran between Dhanushkodi and Talaimannar in Sri Lanka, transporting both goods and travellers across the sea. It was a vibrant place: lots of small hotels, food corners, textile shops, and other retail outlets did brisk business. Even Swami Vivekananda, a great Indian scholar, in Jan 1897, stepped on Indian soil in Dhanushkodi after attending the 'parliament of religions' in the USA. Now, its past glory lies in ruins. There is an interesting story doing the rounds. A local fisherman, Neechal Kali, has seen the top portion of a Ganesha temple, about one kilometre from the shore, which was submerged under the sea after the cyclone. He says he used to play near the temple when he was a young boy and saved many lives during the tidal wave, pulling some people out of the water.

Some old British documents claim there were plans to lay a railway line from Dhanushkodi to Sri Lanka. This place was untouched by progress; nothing much has happened here since the great tragedy. Another initiative was taken when some religious institutions lobbied in 2003. The southern railways sent a project report to the railway ministry and asked them to re-lay a 16-18 kilometre new railway line from Rameshwaram to Dhanushkodi. The fate of that report is still unknown. Earlier, it seemed a distant dream but now there are more chances as the new regime in the centre seems very keen to revive the plans of connectivity.

Returning to my own journey, our driver moved ahead and told us he would halt here again on the way back from the shore. He carried on traversing through the sand dunes for another 20 minutes of bone-jarring journey. It was 6 kilometres of loneliness travelling over bare land. We felt relieved when we got down; I stretched for a while to ease my rattled joints. At first glance, I was astonished to see how empty this place was and at the same time, I thought, what a calm ambience all around. There were 3 more jeeps parked 60-70 metres away from the shore, yet the area looked completely bereft of tourists.

Some people often comment, "There is no land, only water and sand." It seemed true; there was water as far as the naked eye could see. Although it was not far from the hustling and bustling Rameshwaram, the tranquillity and charm of this beach made me feel as if I had stepped into a different world. Unfortunately, there was very little to explore, and the beach was blissfully undemanding. The sand here was so fine that it squeaked under the feet. As I glanced back, I saw a line of footprints that I had left on the wet sand. Apparently, the sand here was punctured by visitors only.

Nonetheless, the waves of 2 seas mingle here and invite you to have a dip. Some young couples were doing the same in the warm seawater.

They were splashing the water on each other, going back and forth in the sea. The water looked beautiful, shimmering like a sheet of ice under the blistering sun. This was the only seashore I have visited in India that was as amazing as I imagined. I saw a distinct difference in the behaviour of the 2 seas; the Indian Ocean looked aggressive with waves rising high, and the Bay of Bengal was unbelievably gentle and calmer.

Unfortunately, this beach was underdeveloped. There weren't any basic facilities like drinking water, lavatories, or eating places, let alone sun loungers or big umbrellas. If it was a sunny hot day or raining, you wouldn't find any shade or man-made shelters. But it was still refreshing to gambol about or have a dip in the shallow waters in the sweltering heat. Because the sea was not deep, I could see some colourful corals, fish, and seaweed while walking in the water.

By now, 2 more small trucks had arrived, and I could see some more visitors on their way. Most of the pilgrims in those trucks were youngsters in their 20s. They looked very cheerful, astonished, and relieved. A couple of them were dusting their faces with hankies while looking around curiously. One young man was pointing out at the sea to his parents while brushing his hair. Out of the blue, I saw 2 European girls walking towards the truck. I swiftly went to them while they were rushing to catch it. Apparently, they were from Sweden: I had never expected to see any Europeans around there, let alone young ladies in their early 20s. They stood on the back lid of the truck, and one of them waved with one hand while holding on to the thick chain of the lid with the other. I felt very happy to see them as if they were from my own city, Newcastle upon Tyne. I wanted to ask them about their experience at this place; sadly, they departed.

I saw some middle-aged pilgrims praying at the spot on the shore where Lord Rama once bathed, and his forces had crossed to Lanka to free his wife from Ravana. I, too, felt the divinity of that place; I touched the sand with reverence where Lord Rama and Lord Hanuman once walked. Then we walked towards the shabby stalls to buy some souvenirs, but they had only a few bottles of water and some bags of potato chips hanging on a small bamboo pole. The late morning was getting hotter, and as there were no shades to protect us from the sun, it was a good time to take our leave.

Although I thoroughly enjoyed every moment on the beach, my mind was still wandering around the deserted town of Dhanushkodi. On the way back to the town, the buried railway track revealed the first glimpse of the 'land that once flourished'. I found it hard to believe the place was once densely populated; I forgot all the jolts in the jeep. It reminded me of someone who described this place as haunting yet appealing, deserted but still full of life, eerie but fascinating. Geographically, Dhanushkodi may be anonymous or unexplored but spiritually, this place occupies a prime place in the minds of Hindus.

My head was spinning with the thought of the horrific cyclone. Many years on, the ill-fated journey and the awful demise of so many lives could not have been forgotten. There was not much for the tourist to pinpoint, largely because there was so little of it left. It was conspicuous by the distinctive features all around the town: a vast wasteland; broken boats on the shores, a few shanty huts selling water bottles, snacks, etc. We spent an hour and a half roaming around the ruins of the ghost town. Shaken to the core, we reached the Dhanushkodi railway station where nothing was left apart from scattered railway tracks and some broken red cement benches, where passengers once waited for trains. There was no ticket office, no tourists, no pilgrims, no fishermen, nothing but sadness.

The thorny bushes and dangerously broken walls prevented us from walking further. In fact, we didn't need to. As we came around, it was peculiar to see a small well with drinking water, just around 30 metres away from the railway station. It is claimed that the water stays cool and sweet in the well that never dries. It showed that 'God is great'. As the well was only around 3 feet deep, a local man helped us to get some water from it with a pitcher that was tied with a thin bamboo stick. Surprisingly, the water was sweet and cool despite a hot sunny day.

Most of the pilgrims told me blatantly that they came to Dhanushkodi to see the Rama Setu only. They had never thought to see the town in disrepair. I witnessed some clear traces of vibrant life and the serene remains of a once prominent and bustling tourist spot. A few buildings had survived the aftermath of the storm for a good number of years. There were unimpressive ruins of what was once a splendid church; a pedestal, which could have been the altar, stood intact. A post office was only a grand red arc; the rest of it was buried in the sand. A school building gave an eerie feeling of a lost civilisation, and a rusted four-pillared structure, possibly a water tank, stood in the middle of this lost land. Some prickly bushes were growing all around the hamlet. It seemed every ruined building hid a story of human agony.

As we walked towards the shore, barely another soul was around. There were a couple of shabby-looking men pulling their dinghy boats. Even the network of my mobile didn't work there, not a bar of phone signal registered. The only sound we could hear was of the waves lapping against the deserted shore. It seemed like a snake and rat-infested area around the spiky bushes. We had to follow an obscure path, near the school building buried in the sand, to arrive back at our jeep. Although there was emptiness, I wanted to gaze around for longer, but I had to bid farewell with a heavy heart.

The roads had been completely taken over by nature. Dhanushkodi might be haunting, daunting, and depressing, yet it was utterly different from any other ruined place in the world I have visited so far.

It was hard to figure out whether it was history, a myth, or both. This tranquil hamlet deserves recognition of its own as it has kept the history alive. Nonetheless, it was a stark reminder of nature's might and the fragility of life.

As we set off back down the precarious track in the dwindling light, I noticed that we were, once again, the only people there apart from an odd fisherman at a distance. Once it was full of hustle and bustle, the noise of ringing bells in the temples, the shouts of various vendors in the busy market, and the celebrations of festivals, but now it was filled with fading memories and uneven sand dunes.

It is advisable to visit this place in groups during the day and return to Rameshwaram before the sun sets as the entire 17–18-kilometre stretch is lonely and scary. A significant police presence to protect the visitors is only situated in the village, Moonram Chathiram. What a memorable ride it was, perhaps too much history for one sunny day.

As we were totally exhausted after such a gruelling day in Dhanushkodi, it was sensible to check out the flow of a cold shower in the hotel in Rameshwaram. I stretched my aching legs on the bed before venturing out to the local market to buy some knick-knacks where, amazingly, I ran into the same 2 Swedish girls who were in Dhanushkodi in the morning. I was moved by their knowledge of The Ramayana. They described Lord Rama and Lord Hanuman in a nutshell. As they were in a hurry to go, I took their e-mail addresses to ask about their interests in other related sites. Unfortunately, they haven't replied to me so far.

SITA MATA CIRCUIT

If Rama is the protagonist of The Ramayana, Sita Mata is certainly the heart and soul of the text. The progression of the narration of The Ramayana revolves around Sita; from birth to marriage, from her parents' dwellings to Rama's family, and from the abduction by Ravana to life in Lanka during exile, as well as her last days, are unique and pivotal incidents.

It is believed that Sita was born at Panaura Dham, located in the District of Sitamarhi in Bihar. When King Janak was ploughing the field to please the Rain God, Indra, to pray for rainwater as the state was facing drought, the plough struck an earthen pot and Sita came out of it. According to another school of thought, the actual birthplace of Sita is Janakpur, the capital of the Mithila Kingdom of Raja Janak, which is in present-day Nepal. At that time, there were no borders between the current State of Bihar and Nepal; therefore, the 2 cities were not separate as they are only 50 miles apart. The Janakpur temple is splendid and very beautiful, but across the border, the Panaura temple is older and culturally rich, so both have the same level of importance in terms of spirituality. The people of Janakpur recognise Sita, the baby, as a divine gift to King Janak and his queen Sunayana. As Sita was found in a furrow, they named her Sita - a Sanskrit word for furrow.

On my maiden journey to Nepal in November 2011, Kathmandu was the only entry point. In the early morning, with my body clock 5.45 hours ahead of local time, I was tired but wide awake. The dawn was made even more special by the undeniably picturesque view all around; the sun was rising from behind the valley, and the bright light on the verdant mountains on the other side looked fabulous. We spent the first day visiting the local monuments, including the Pashupati Nath Shiva temple. Even though it was busy and noisy, I could still feel tranquillity and sensual calm. It was easy to become familiar with the country where the culture and cuisine were nearly the same, and Hindi was spoken widely.

JANAKPUR DHAM VIA DEV GHAT

Next morning, we set off to explore the main monument, Janaki Dham, but decided to visit Dev Ghat on the way. After an early lunch at Narayangarh, it took half an hour to reach Dev Ghat. This is the place where the Kali Gandaki and Trishuli rivers converge to form the Narayani River. As the confluence of rivers is considered sacred by Hindus, large numbers of pilgrims visit here for ritual bathing.

A fable has it that this is the place where Mother Earth opened to receive Sita. It was a tranquil place where a small temple was tucked in the valley across the river. Within the parameters, behind the rocky hill was a large crack that opened up to accept Sita. It was surrounded by the unspoilt wilderness of heavily wooded mountains.

It took a few minutes to adjust to the peculiar atmosphere on the banks of the rivers. I was astonished to see 2 corpses burning on the pyres side by side, and another one wrapped in a shroud waiting to go. At the same time, only a few metres away, the local families were cooking fresh food to relish some sort of ceremony. Children were rejoicing in the atmosphere, playing with balloons and other toys. There could be a reason for burning the dead bodies by the banks of the river as some Hindus believe that by dying there at the confluence of the rivers, one can break the cycle of rebirth and attain salvation. Before going to Janakpur, we went to see some other shrines towards the bus stand.

After 15 minutes, we were driving along a scenic road with barely a soul in sight. The river was gently flowing alongside the road. Some tinned roof houses lined the hillside, and the paddy fields looked fabulous on the symmetrical stepped mountain slope; the views were scenic. I felt tired in the uncomfortable vehicle as it would not go beyond 45 miles an hour. A couple of samosas and a cup of tea revived my energy for the rest of the journey.

As we passed the cemented gate of Janakpur town, the narrow road and streets looked busy with motorbikes and three-wheelers. It looked as if everyone was heading towards the prime site, Janaki Dham. Most of the pilgrims seemed to have arrived from across the borders from the State of Bihar as they did not need any visas.

Janki Dham temple is the most famous place for Hindus in Nepal. The queen of Orchha, Vrisha Bhanu, built this temple in 1910. It was completed in a mixed style of Islam and Rajput domes. The three-story structure is 50 metres high. A golden statue of Sita is enshrined here. It is believed that the poet Sanyasi Shur Kishore Das found this golden statue during the 17th century.

Janakpur in the Eastern Terai is one of the oldest cities of Nepal. In ancient times, Mithila was the capital of Videha, and King Janak ruled the Empire. The major significance is the Janaki temple, which sometimes the local people compare with the importance of the Rama Temple in Ayodhya.

As I entered the vicinity of the temple, my happiness knew no bounds. I was at the place where Sita once spent her childhood and played all around. The huge temple building has a magnetic appeal as it was built with white marble and is surrounded by octagonal parapets and crowned with marble Chatteris. The large silver gate in the inner sanctum signifies its vastness. It was significantly famous and a feast for the eyes.

VIVAH MANDAP

As we went further to the right, a beautiful rectangular structure of white marble was adorning the place. It is believed that Lord Rama married Sita here after he broke the ancient Shiva bow in 2 pieces. Therefore, it is called Vivah Mandap. Inside the marriage pavilion, the idols of Rama and Sita sitting on a couch in wedding attire with golden crowns on their heads enhanced the sight of the place. On both sides, the idols of sages and family members depicted the marriage ceremony. A few metres ahead, we visited some more temples of various Gods and strolled around the temple premises.

A tangle of streets, alleyways, and roads follows the city's ancient history. The inner town was full of shops selling articles related to the deities and souvenirs. Small eateries were full of customers. It was fascinating to meet a German girl in the front garden of the hotel. She was a doctor employed by the World Health Organisation conducting a Polio injection spree in Nepal. She told me that although the job assigned to her was in Pokhara, a much popular place with foreign travellers, she always preferred to spend her holidays in this area as it had a feel of authentic Nepal.

Janakpur was small enough to walk from one place to another and large enough to spend a few days. I loved the energy, buzz, and sheer scale of the city.

DHANUSH DHAM

Dhanush Dham, 'House of bow', is the second most famous site in Janakpur. It is situated 18 kilometres to the northeast. According to the epic, this was the place where the remains of the divine bow fell after Rama broke it in 2 and proved himself worthy of Sita.

We hired a three-wheeler to view the site. The driver took a short cut through the villages and reached there in half an hour. It didn't look like a temple from outside. As its name was stated on the wall and the structure looked large enough to be a holy place, I felt I was on top of the world. In fact, there was a small temple on the other side. As we entered Dhanush Dham, there were the remains of Shiva's bow in the form of an arc beside an ancient tree. Most of the bow was covered with garlands of marigold and holy red thread. The priest waited for a few more pilgrims to gather around before explaining the history. Some devotees sat on a raised floor, and some stood beside the wall to listen to the tales. After relating the incidents, he pointed at the broken bow and said, "This material is unique. It appears to grow a fraction of millimetres every year. Even the scientists cannot figure out the reason." The great description of the bow ceremony was followed by an outburst of joyous applause by the pilgrims. The enthusiasm of the visitors from India made the atmosphere livelier.

SITA RETURNING TO 'MOTHER EARTH' IN SITAMARHI (IN UTTAR PRADESH)

It is believed that this temple is the spot where Sita descended to the Earth when she desired while she was living in a forest of Sitamarhi. I don't know whether it is a sheer coincidence or God's will that there are 2 places known as Sitamarhi, and both are related to Sita. Both places are in India but in different States. One where Sita was found by King Janak while ploughing the fields in Bihar, and the other where Sita returned to the lap of Mother Earth in the Poorvanchal region of Uttar Pradesh.

Some historians described other places too where Sita was taken back to Mother Earth. Bithoor, near Kanpur, Valmiki Nagar in Bihar, Rama Tirath in Punjab, and a place in Jharkhand claim similar sites. I witnessed the place that was earmarked in The Ramayana, the temple in Sitamarhi. The author of Rama Chrit Manas, Tulsi Das, had visited the place for 3 days while travelling between Kashi and Prayagraj. He described this location between Baripur and Digpur; the 2 villages still exist and testify to the location. It was supposed to be 64 Kos (approximately 3.7 Kilometres in a Kos) towards Dakshin (south) from Ayodhya, and it was possible to reach by chariot in a day.

The entire vicinity of the temple looked enchanting and peaceful, but the prime temple of Sita was outstanding. The temple was situated in the middle of a small lake with beautiful gardens all around. As we passed the footbridge and entered the shrine, the atmosphere was so serene and calm that I could hear my own breathing. The tales of Sita's life depicted fabulously. Even the ceiling was decorated with glossy colours in such a way that I could not stare at it for long; the murals of Sita adorned the place. Half an hour wasn't long enough to grasp the beauty and the history before my eyes. The small statues of various Gods, explaining their tales all around the outer walls of the temple, were equally charming.

The stairs from inside the temple hall took me to the basement, where the depiction of the last moments of Sita opened my eyes in sorrow and my mouth in despair. The soft white marble statue of Sita, in a walking posture on a lotus in the middle of the glowing pyre of stones, was a focal point in the shrine. It looked very attractive behind the glass frame. The hall was white-washed, creating a sombre atmosphere. It showed the scenes reverently. Her long hair was waving, and the face looked cool and calm. I felt like weeping in condolence. Had I stayed there a bit longer, I would have literally sobbed in that ambience.

It was very lively with local visitors outside the vicinity. A huge statue of Hanuman was the main attraction as children were enjoying the cave at the bottom. We hired a three-wheeler to go to Valmiki Ashram near the River Ganga, though it was only 600 metres away. The place looked ancient but quiet. As we passed the gate where some scriptures depicted scenes from The Ramayana, a couple of children aged 7 or 8 came over and explained the story behind them in chaste Hindi with pure Sanskrit words and showed the old Peepal tree under which Sita used to pray. I witnessed some more shrines related to the era before leaving the historical site.

PLACES TO VISIT IN SRI LANKA

JOURNEY TO LANKA

My desire to visit Sri Lanka took many shapes and forms before I set off; mythology and history played a pivotal role. We embarked on a late evening flight from Mumbai to Colombo in February 2011. It was an exhilarating beginning, not because it was my maiden journey to Sri Lanka but also a first trip to explore The Ramayana sites. I was very enthusiastic and full of energy. My 90kg body was fixed in the aisle seat, yet I couldn't care less if there wasn't enough leg space or if I was crammed into the seat! I had the same feelings as I had in my childhood when I was squashed into a rickshaw seat along with my 4 siblings on the way to the town fair; only food and rides danced in front of my eyes.

As the Purser of the flight strolled in the aisle, I humbly asked, "Is it feasible to look at the cockpit..., if possible?"

He paused and said, "I can't promise. I shall speak to the captain and let you know."

After a few minutes, he came up and said, "You'll have to wait until all the passengers leave the aircraft."

"Excellent, thanks to you very much," I appreciated his efforts.

Although I was curious to peep into the captain's cabin, my mind was visualising The Ramayana sites. Before I could conclude anything, we landed on the soil that used to be called Golden Lanka, where the mighty King Ravana ruled with prowess over Gods, humans, and demons.

As I waited in the plane, Mr. Purser, as he promised, took me to the cockpit of the aircraft. I caught an enticing glimpse of various lit up metres all around the dashboard; it was fascinating to see how the captain controls all the equipment at the same time. No wonder, this specific job is conducted by selective persons. It was a great start to my maiden project.

I wasn't aware of the unusually chaotic upheaval of arriving in the middle of the night; long queues to go through the under-staffed immigration desks seemed like another hour's less sleep. Fortunately, it didn't take long as we did not need a visa in 2011.

Generally, the first thing that pops into any Hindu's mind when visiting Sri Lanka is where did Ravana live, where did he hide Sita, where did Hanuman set fire to the palaces, and what Ashok Vatika looks like, etc.

The importance of Sri Lanka can be adjudged from the fact that The Ramayana began with Ayodhya in India but climaxed at Lankapura, the capital city of Lanka. Sri Lanka is the only place after India where most of the incidents related to The Ramayana took place. Around the end of the last century, The Ramayana sites were totally off-limits to Indian tourists. It became alive in the most enthralling way when the Sri Lankan Government began to promote these places to Hindus worldwide.

In the middle of the night, my mind was still doing rounds of Ravana's Lanka, though I knew it would be impossible to witness that era in today's public life. I was lying in bed, looking at the streaks of light coming from the side of the curtains on the ceiling, keeping the dark at bay. Sleep was miles away; I was fixated on.

For some reason, I never took Ravana as an antagonist. I thought his karma made him take haughty decisions to abduct Sita. Ravana was a learnt Brahmin. According to Hindu mythology, Ravana was born to a great sage, Vishrava, and his wife, Princess Kaikesi.

Lanka was an idyllic city, created by the celestial architect, Vishwakarma, at the behest of Lord Shiva. It was Kuber's – the half-brother of Ravana and the treasurer of the Gods – dwelling when Ravana demanded Lanka for himself or threatened to take over by force.

It is believed in Sri Lankan folklore that Lanka enjoyed great advancements in medicine and science. The Pushpa-Vimana – aircraft – which Ravana used is held as an example of great scientific achievement during his regime. Above all, Ravana was a great physician and author who wrote several books on Ayurveda as well as Ravana Sanhita, an anthology of Hindu astrology. Ravana was the most revered devotee of Lord Shiva; the Stotram – Shiva Tandav Satotram – was created by him; he had an intense knowledge of music. Ravana's ten-headed person description might be a reference to his vast knowledge and intelligence. Even Rama, after mortally injuring Ravana, sent Lakshmana to him to learn some wisdom.

Valmiki's Ramayana painted Ravana as a tyrant of mighty powers who was holding the Gods at random. Ravana was one of the most powerful beings ever to roam on Earth. However, he is still considered an antagonist in India; although, in a few places, he is worshipped in some temples.

MUNESHWARAM AND MUNAVERI

After arriving in the dark last night, I could not figure out that we were staying in the hotel on the western coast in Negombo. The next morning, we enjoyed the exotic breakfast while watching the waves coming fast and dying suddenly in the fine sands of our hotel complex; it was a comfortable 28 degrees centigrade. No sooner had we arrived in the lobby, the chauffeur-cum-guide whisked us across the Chillaw-Puton road in a car. After a twenty-minute drive, we were enjoying the neat corridor of amazingly tall palm trees along the roadside. As our car meandered along the coastal route, my guide outlined most of the tour.

He said, "As you want to uncover many mythological and historical places, it will be a mistake to rush; it won't be good to cram them into a short trip. I shall try my best to cover as much as I can."

I remained enthralled for the whole tour. As our driver knew that this was my first trip to Sri Lanka, he took it upon himself to don the role of an intelligent guide. Occasionally, I asked him about the pronunciation of a few places that I had researched; he happily explained them.

At first glance, the lush landscapes filled with palm trees along the beach looked stunning. It seemed they were planted to shade the travellers and local workforce when the road was made; they were in good numbers at regular intervals, the meadows of short grass around them looked providing the cool effect. The vista of wind rustling the fronds of palm trees kept me hooked to the scenery. I was partly surprised because I had an image of a war-torn country.

We drove past a few ladies walking in a row with the green produce balanced on their heads. There was a little local traffic on the way to the Muneshwaram temple. I felt a bit irritated when the road was clear, and the speedometer needle was not crossing the 50 km mark. Just before entering the town, I noticed some policemen directing and controlling the vehicles from the central podiums. The journey to Chillaw was so picturesque that we did not realise it took nearly 2 hours for 35 km. The thwack noise of a cricket ball from local men playing in the field near Chillaw caught my attention.

As we entered the town, I saw the Gopuram of the Muneshwaram temple looming large over the complex; it was hard to miss. It is believed that the Muneshwaram temple predates The Ramayana era.

When Lord Rama, after his victorious battle, left for Ayodhya in Vimana, he felt he was being followed by a Brahmasthi Dosham – a malevolent black shadow, a dark cloud capable of taking life. When the Vimana entered the Muneshwaram airspace, there was no disturbance. Rama noticed that the Brahmasthi Dosham was not following him. Rama stopped the Vimana at this juncture in Muneshwaram complex. Rama prayed to Lord Shiva and his consort, Parvati, and asked for a remedy. Shiva and Parvati appeared and blessed Rama. Shiva advised him to install and pray to the Lingam near the banks of River Oya Deduru at Munaveri to get rid of the Brahmasthi Dosham for killing a Brahmin King. The folklore believes that Rama was asked to install 4 Lingams, including Thiru Koneshwaram in Trincomalee, Thiru Koteshwaram in Mannar, and Rameshwaram in India. But my research showed that Lord Rama prayed at Koneshwaram and Koteshwaram at some stage during his stay in Lanka and installed a Lingam only in Rameshwaram.

There were many shops and stalls selling a large variety of fruits and flowers as offerings. Every vendor tried to sell some sort of packages as offerings; we could not get away fast enough. We walked past a stunning wooden chariot on the left which they used for the processions during festivals like Shivaratri. The priest conducted a prayer in the main Shiva temple in the middle of a vast complex. We adored all the murals and statues of the deities while circling the main shrine; they all looked impressive.

After paying our obeisance, we set off for the Munaveri temple that was around 5 kilometres. Without the help of a guide, we wouldn't have found this place. After passing the River Oya Deduru, the temple premises were on the left, where we could easily miss a small signboard stating the name.

I was surprised that the outlook of the area and the temple complex was very rugged or rather ignored for such a significant Hindu revering place. There was a dusty path to the temple in 2011, but a slight improvement of a tarred road seemed a big achievement in 2017. It was one of the oldest Shiva temples in Sri Lanka but without the striking beauty from outside. The sight of the temple was dull with decaying surroundings. The thrill of arriving somewhere so special where Lord Rama himself installed and worshipped the Shiva Lingam dampened the spirit; in my mind's eye, I had savoured a grand appearance. As we went further, the cemented gate before the temple precinct assured its importance. The small temple inside the walled premises was quite clean and charming.

The Lingam here in Munaveri temple was the first one installed and prayed to by Lord Rama, and to date, the Lingam is called Ramalinga Shivam. Rameshwaram in India is the only other Lingam in the world named after Lord Rama.

We timed it well. The priest was coming out of his room to conduct the evening aarti. A Sri Lankan couple with a child from Birmingham was also waiting for its opening. Some other local lady devotees helped the priest to set up the puja pots for aarti. I felt elated that I started my first trip with the blessings of Lord Shiva and Lord Rama from this revered place. It gave me a monumental boost to my spirit and energy.

RAMBODA

As we left Negombo, I put my mind into arithmetic mode. I concluded that even if the traffic stayed as it was in the city during rush hours, we should be in our hotel by 1.30 pm. By the time we have our lunch and a bit of rest, the temple of Hanuman for the evening aarti would be open.

The Ramayana trail began to make more impact when I saw a yellow temple of Hanuman on top of the hill before entering the village. I was as excited to visit Bhakta Hanuman Temple as when I first visited it on 18 February 2011. I considered this temple the most important starting place for our tour in many ways. First and foremost, the reason to pay my obeisance in this temple was that it was in the area where Hanuman landed and located Sita for the first time. The other reason was that this part of Lanka has been described in Sunder Kanda in The Ramayana; hence, a good omen to commence the tour.

Barely an hour after arriving at my hotel, I was ready to hit the trail with the camera in my shoulder bag. We reached the car park in less than 10 minutes. It seemed there were few visitors at the time, but the vast swathes of empty car park were a testament to the fact that a good number of pilgrims must visit here. The Hanuman Temple stood atop a hill in splendid isolation. As we walked past some shops selling offerings and souvenirs, we followed the steep road to the temple; it was perfect timing as the priest was getting the puja brass pot ready for the evening aarti. A sixteen-foot-tall statue in a standing posture, carved out of black granite, was in front of our eyes. It looked fabulous.

There were a few families in the sanctum sanctorum with offerings in their hands. The priest began to chant some mantras while ringing the bell. As we were enjoying the spiritual ambience, the priest came up to me and gave some prasad. I asked for his permission to take some photographs, as on my first trip they did not allow this, maybe due to the reason that they were bathing the deity and changing his outfit; but, to see the deity having Sanan while chanting the mantras was soothing to the eyes.

As my guide Dushan had made an appointment with Amma, Acharya Brahmacharini Thivyawadani, who was managing the place, we went to meet her after taking some photographs. She elaborated on the importance of the place.

"This place is under the management of the Chinmaya Mission of Sri Lanka. It was Gurudev, Swami Tejomay Ananda's Sankalpa – commitment, when he visited Sri Lanka in 1980, to set up a spiritual centre at Ramboda. Chinmaya Mission purchased 10 acres of land in 1981 at Wevanden Hills. Guru Devji named the land 'Ramboda' and consecrated the temple on 8th April 2001, by performing Maha Kumbhabhishaken – major puja. Now, even the Sri Lankan Government approves this place in their tourism information as a Ramayana site."

Annapurni, a vegetarian restaurant in the complex, looked stunning on the eastern hill. Although the light-yellow temple and its immediate green surroundings on the hill-top were the essence of the complex, the newly built structure, Chinmaya Niwas, on the left near the entrance looked fabulous in the middle of nature. This two-floor building contained 14 rooms; each room was named after the characters of The Ramayana including Vibhishana, Sugreeva, etc. A very useful office, cafe, and bookshop were set up on the right side, in front of the stone steps before ascending to the temple.

The surroundings offered wonderfully rolling countryside around the hill that had escaped the attention of tourist hordes. The solitude was a welcome antidote from the city madness. The tranquillity and ambience were so staggering that I wanted to stay in their accommodation for a few days, but my itinerary did not allow it; I made up my mind there and then to return soon.

Looking around from the temple hill was bliss. The green forest below, the mountains in the distance, offered wonderful views of the Kotmale reservoir. Looking across the plunging valleys arced around the reservoir made me think of how nature had architected the entire scenery. As if that were not enough, the landscape on the other side looked astonishing too; the mountains soared up in such a way that the view of the hills appeared to depict the image of Hanuman in a lying posture.

I noticed a good number of school children in white uniform, along with their teachers, walking up the road in broken queues. Walking barefoot on the stone pavement in the hot sun was a testing time for the young feet; the children who walked in the shady area laughed hysterically at others' jumping skills on the hot surface. It was a pleasing atmosphere in an utterly quiet place.

After a heavy rain overnight, in the morning, the clouds still looked swirling at a distance. However, the blue sky broke through every so often and revealed lush green meadows at the base of the mountains; the sun was trying and failing to come out. At times, sunrays shone brightly on the top edge of the mountain, but the lower valley looked dull. The whole scenario drew me to the balcony.

As I was getting ready to go to the temple before breakfast, I heard Janak slamming and bolting the door. There were a few monkeys on the balcony, probably looking for something for their breakfast. Janak threw some bananas and leftover snacks in the corner; they nearly snatched them out of her hand. It was interesting to watch them peeling the banana and throwing the peel carelessly onto the tinned roof. Anyhow, it was expected in Hanuman's own area.

As we arrived on the temple hill, the environment felt blissfully calm and empty; the fully blossomed gardens looked fabulously fresh. The scent of flowers wafted through the air; dew-kissed rose petals soothed the eyes, while sunshine on the body in the cool morning acted like a healing balm. The serene location enhanced the spirituality.

The time was fast approaching for the morning puja and aarti. As I had requested the priest the previous evening to conduct a special puja, he chanted some mantras after tying the holy thread around our wrists; he performed it with full conviction.

The priest asked us to visit the meditation hall below the temple. We calmly strolled around the place for a few minutes. It was filled with pure holiness where I could hear my own breathing. The tranquil ambience brought out my meditating intentions, but a lack of patience deterred me. Being a devotee of Hanuman, it gave me mountainous pleasure.

As we were waiting for the lift to go down to the breakfast hall, I noticed a fabulous monstrous waterfall in the left corner. It was cascading the water from the nearby mountain, rushing over grey smooth stones and gurgling from under the main road into the deep gorge. Last night, I could hardly make out where the noise of falling water was coming from, but the morning light gave me a pleasant view. The Ramboda falls curled and trembled down the gorge lined with steep valleys. It was a perfect place to start the day after the morning prayers.

The air in the large veranda where they had set up the buffet breakfast was scented with the aromas of freshly cooked food. I reserved a table next to the dwarf wall, where we could lean over to the beautiful garden below and have a good view of the waterfall. While chugging down chilled fresh watermelon juice, I watched the view of the dark green tea plantation hills, cascading their waters slowly into the waterfall; I was so engrossed with the scenery that the jam on the toast landed on my upper lip. After a fruitful morning, we were ready to explore the Sita Temple and its surroundings in Nuwara Eliya.

NUWARA ELIYA

As we drove past the gurgling waterfalls of Ramboda, the driver followed a short cut route to the city of Nuwara Eliya. Immediately, I noticed some dramatic changes in landscapes; the tall mountains on one side and the deep gorge on the other with tea plantations spread across the valleys. The closer we got to the mountains, the more spectacular the hill country became. It was fascinating from the word 'go'. Every turn in the road was a camera shot, but I did not want to stop; we wanted to reach the city as soon as possible.

Unfortunately, or fortunately, just before the city, on the hill, our car broke down. It had overheated due to the ascending drive. We came out and went under the temporary shelter on a small cliff alongside the road. It felt good to roam around in the fresh air. As I looked across, there was a combination of a green carpet of tea plantations rolling deep down near the ravine and the compact dwellings of tea workers densely located at the bottom of the green hills. The deep green tea plantations were so bright in places that they often looked fluorescent during the sunny morning. My eyes gazed at the sight of women in greyish outfits plucking the buds and leaves and putting them in the sacks on their backs. It was amazing to see their hands carrying out routine work while they were talking and walking around the bushes in parallel lines.

The moment we entered the Nuwara Eliya hills, I was instantly energised. I forgot the slight dizziness that I had experienced on the zigzag ascent. The colonial history was evident as soon as the car entered the cemented gate of Nuwara Eliya city. A solitary man pulling his golf trolley on a vast velvety golf course on the left greeted us. It felt like being in Scotland. People often refer to this part of the country as the mini-England of eastern Sri Lanka.

Ashok and Indu were very keen to visit the Sita Temple as they had seen the shrine on television broadcasting The Ramayana sites. Although it was a bright day, the strong rays of the sun could not heat the tall tree-lined avenues. It has been over 50 years since the British departed; however, the town revealed the legacy they left behind. Many colonial houses with large allotments along the roadside were apparent. There was virtually no traffic on the road; the Victoria Park on the left looked busy with the children riding the horses.

SITA TEMPLE

As we reached the most awaited place, the Sita kovil, the landscape looked like the perfect place for the Gods. Nuwara Eliya is an uncelebrated city in terms of religious significance, but the Sita Temple here has great mythological importance for the people of India. It is located on the road to Badulla. The place is treated with enduring devotion by Hindus as this is the only temple outside India that is dedicated to Goddess Sita. Unequivocally, this shrine is the most popular site on The Ramayana trail in Sri Lanka. Due to the presence of the footprints of Hanuman behind the temple, there is lots of evidence that this was a part of the mythical Ashok Vatika, meaning a large garden.

I felt distinctly happy to visit such a temple again that retained a character and soul of its own. The temple itself was in incredible settings. The Dravidian style shrine was built around Ashok Vatika and set in idyllic countryside beside a stream where Goddess Sita used to bathe and pray for Rama to free her from the clutches of Ravana. It is overlooked by clusters of trees and set against a backdrop of sweeping hills. The stream, known as Sita Ganga, running behind the temple, appeared calm and serene.

As we went down the concrete steps in the temple complex, I was immediately captivated, and the spiritual vibes made me feel even more energetic. It was a small but vibrant place with a few revered sites. It reminded me of my school days when the teacher used to tell this story in Hindi lessons. I found it to be just as I imagined it when I read about the place in the textbooks. The temple itself was ornately carved. On the ceiling, vividly painted scenes from The Ramayana were quite attractive. The walls were covered with the murals of mythical figures. Lord Krishna in blue was portrayed showing his skills in playing the flute. Some places were very cleverly painted showing Lord Vishnu with his consort and representing all his avatars.

The main priest was busy doing puja for other pilgrims; he had a brass pot with camphor blocks burning in one hand and the offerings in the other. Incense clouds wafted through the air from the small temple.

In the meantime, a couple of staff members came up and showed us a majestic brass plaque of embossed pictures of Rama, Sita, Lakshmana, and Hanuman in an elegant maroon velvety box that could be transformed into an impressive frame. They had commemorated a special puja, Maha-Kumbabishekam on the 18th of May 2016 and released them as a souvenir. It looked so sophisticated that Ashok and I bought them immediately.

The main priest took our offerings and performed a puja for us. Although I knew some of the history, I was keen to learn more about the significance of the place.

The priest was courteous, and he said, "This place is known as Sita kovil, meaning temple. During The Ramayana era, it was a part of Ashok Vatika where Ravana kept Sita as a prisoner. There are 2 temples. One, close to the riverbank, is enshrined with the 3 black idols of Rama, Sita, and Lakshmana that were found in a river more than a century ago. The other one on the right is a Sita Temple. It is a new structure with new statues of the same deities. The prominent rock on the riverbank is where Sita meditated and prayed."

His evidence convinced us that the episode in The Ramayana texts indeed took place here.

He continued, "This is not a myth, but a history where Sita was imprisoned. Hanuman's footprints validate the theory. The land and mountains have been untouched by intensive development and are supposed to remain the same as when they featured in The Ramayana."

The priest discreetly pointed out the black-soiled hill across the river.

He said, "Take a look at the colour of the soil; it is black. When Hanuman got Sita's permission to satisfy his desire to eat some fruits from the gardens, he uprooted and burnt many trees. Since then, an area of 5 kilometres still has black soil. If you see the colour of the soil across the road; it's red."

Apparently, Ashok Vatika was the place where Hanuman met Sita for the first time and Ravana approached Sita for the last time, still in the hope of obtaining her consent to be his principal queen. Sita's rejection made Ravana so furious that he ran towards Sita to kill her, but Mandodari, Ravana's wife, intervened. Ravana gave Sita one month to yield to him, or she would face certain death. Hanuman, while sitting hidden between the branches of the tree, watched all that happened in the grove. When Hanuman appeared before Sita with folded hands and praised Rama, she looked at the strange monkey and thought this could be another ploy by Ravana to deceive her. Hanuman quickly presented the ring given by Rama and convinced her that he was Rama's envoy. This was the area where Hanuman deliberately uprooted many trees and killed hordes of demons. Consequently, Ravana sent his son, Akshay Kumar, to kill him, but he was no match for Hanuman's sheer strength; hence, he was killed. Ravana wanted to see the creature that had created so much havoc in the kingdom. He sent his older son, Indrajeet, to capture him. In fact, Hanuman got himself arrested so that he could reach the royal chamber of Ravana.

There was a small steel bridge on the Sita Ganga and the idols of Sita receiving a ring from Hanuman, a token Lord Rama sent. When Janak and I visited in 2011, there was no bridge or access to the footmarks. It was too dangerous to cross over the gushing waters of the river. Mischievous monkeys were present all around the temple, jumping from one wall to another. Occasionally, they made faces and showed tongues knowingly while eating the snatched items from the pilgrims. As I tried to make a face in return, a male growled and chased me. I ran hastily into the car without looking back. Surprisingly, I did not spot any monkeys like these the second time.

I stood on the bridge and gazed around. It was a fantastic experience to witness the flat rock where Hanuman's footprints were evident. The yellow marks on the circular depressions depicted his presence. According to the folklore, the footprints were formed when Hanuman danced merrily after meeting Sita. A stream flowing tirelessly under the bridge was eye-catching. I was not only admiring the ambience but also trying to figure out how beautiful this landscape would have been during The Ramayana period. For a few moments, I floated in the sea of that era and relished the history.

We were ready for the hunt for vegetarian food. The driver took us to the city centre; it had retained a distinctive look. Remnants of the British era still dominated in the form of a bank building, local corporation office, and post office etc. A fabulously rich legacy looked attractive and pleasing; the old buildings blended with the contemporary structures. It was small enough to walk around and become familiar within half a day and large enough to spend a few days there.

The small restaurant was jam-packed with locals, a good sign for good food. It was the same sort of place as in India where they serve only snacks including savouries and sweet meal courses. I could murder many of them on the spot as I was craving some spicy dishes.

As we entered the small sitting area, a few men were enjoying their snacks at the different tables; they all had the same thali with 12 pieces of different kinds of food, including large potato balls, samosas, and vada, etc. I could not stop giggling as it seemed far more than enough for a single person. I did not think they could eat all that, but surprisingly they cleared the thali. When we asked the waiter to bring a plate of samosas each, which generally contains 2 pieces, he brought out the same thali for us; Ashok and I burst into laughter.

The waiter said, "Eat whatever you like out of the various items, the rest we take back, and you pay only for what you consume."

Janak and Indu joined us. The situation was so hysterical that the water began to come out of my eyes. Ashok could only finish 2. The local customers looked at us but could not figure out the reason for our laughter. The system seemed unhygienic but was good enough to satisfy our needs. My belly would have revolted if we had gone without them. I relished a few vadas with coconut chutney and a cup of tea.

As we strolled towards the car, the locals seemed relaxed, happy, and less stressed. In fact, I was seduced by this hill station's exotic charm from the moment I set foot on its land.

As we drove past Victoria Park, it reminded me of my stay in 2011 in a hotel on the hill across Gregory Lake. It was a private mansion converted into a hotel and looked very attractive. The location was simply fabulous; the view of the mountains towards Adam's Peak looked splendid while the landscapes around the lake made the location of the hotel perfect. It appealed to us more after a hectic day's travel from Kandy. We chilled out in the small garden. After a well-deserved cup of tea and some pakoras that they had prepared on order, the cold breeze compelled me to enjoy an afternoon power nap. This rare experience was so glorious that it was easy to imagine that the rest of the world did not exist.

We thought it was appropriate to spend some time at Gregory Lake. The calm was perfect, and the sunshine brilliant, not very hot, not very cold. Even though it was a popular spot for local picnickers, there was a relaxing feel of peace as we strolled around the newly developed area of the lake.

We sat down on the bench while adoring the natural beauty. It was good to see some butterflies flittering from one plant to another. Children were running around and shouting; parents made no efforts to restrict them. Some playgrounds and pathways looked delightfully attractive and popular with the native people. An older woman with a sun-creviced face was busy on her mobile in an Australian accent, while her partner seemed to be having a siesta on the grass under the sun. As the shadows lengthened on the lawns, we decided to set off towards our hotel on the hill.

Yogesh and Tripta went to their room for a while, but Janak and I stayed back in the tiny lobby because I fancied a dose of caffeine. When Yogesh came down, the driver asked if he desired any beer or spirits as he wanted to chill out after a long day's drive. Yogesh agreed to have a taste of the local produce. I ordered some coffee with pakoras, but the chef in the hotel didn't have time to make any such snacks. After nursing a quick beer, Yogesh looked happier and more talkative. Better still, he washed down some peanuts with a glass of the much underestimated local drink and told some cracking old-time stories. I was quite content with a couple of black coffees and his jokes, which he had told many times over.

The novelty soon wore off. Virtually, there was nothing available in the kitchen to cook for the vegetarians; a few odd onions and potatoes were showing their age, and the fridge was empty. As Janak and Tripta went into the kitchen, the chef, without any assistance, was literally in tears. They offered to help him in making Kadhi and rice for dinner as we had arranged some gram flour for the pakoras earlier. The relieved chef said that he hadn't slept for the last 3 days. We had to wait for an hour and a half for our own cooked food. A few more residents, including a honeymoon couple from Mumbai, appreciated the food. Similarly, for breakfast, stale bread, half a jar of jam, and runny butter were served in front of us. Was there any fruit or cereals? What!!! How delightful, eh.

I had a nasty surprise when the manager handed over the bill, charging the full amount for the dinner that Janak and Tripta cooked. Even after the driver's intervention, we still had to pay a fair bit of the invoice. To say the least, we bought the stuff, we cooked and served ourselves, and paid for it too. Wow! That is why they say, all that glitters is not gold.

DIVURUMPOLA

Divurumpola is a very important place in the context of The Ramayana, but sadly, pilgrims seldom make it this far. Yet, my intentions were crystal clear, and we were on the way to witness the site where Sita had to undergo a fire-test incident to prove her chastity.

It was only a half-hour drive from the Sita Temple, but the landscapes along the entire route enticed us to go at a turtle's pace. En route, I wanted to explore the Hakgala botanical gardens, but time constraints made me skip it for the time being. However, I could see the towering mountains, which looked inaccessible, as the backdrop, and a cluster of beautiful ridges underlying the hill-top suburbs. The lower area was a botanical garden on a steep hill. It is believed that the entire area was part of Ravana's Ashok Vatika.

We passed some pitch-roofed brick and stone houses that evoked the British Raj; several thatched houses with eye-catching allotments passed by. They had cultivated vegetables in such a symmetrical way that we had to slow down to appreciate them.

I was in a sombre mood when I thought about Sita who spent a full year in hellish conditions, and then she had to undergo a fire-test to prove her chastity. As we reached the dusty car park, I thought the driver had taken us to a different place as there was a beautiful Buddha temple in a tranquil suburb. As we came out, a senior citizen with a small copybook and pen rushed towards us. Before I could ask anything, he told us to pay the required entry fee to enter the place behind the temple. We followed him.

An unfinished wooden statue of Hanuman under the shabby tinned roof greeted us. Immediately next to it was a small temple of Goddess Sita. He opened the shrine and switched on the various lights. The Goddess Sita's statue and a mural depicting her walking through the fire were fabulously lit.

It is believed that Sita, adorned with flower jewellery, was taken in a palanquin before Rama after the victory over Ravana. She was overcome with emotion after meeting Rama after such a long time.

The place of the 'fire-testing' was initially fenced and walled to protect it from the wild surroundings. Then the sapling from the Anuradhapura Bodhi tree was planted as a mark of respect for the site. A small dagoba was subsequently built under the Bodhi tree. The temple depicted the paintings of The Ramayana epic. We strolled and cherished the tranquil atmosphere for a while in the large open area around the tree.

SIGIRIYA ROCK - RAVANA'S PALACE

As we left Kandy for the iconic monument of Sri Lanka, Sigiriya rock, also known as Lion Rock, I wanted to visit a temple in Matale on the way, but the driver missed the turning. We carried on to the Dambulla Caves, but the severe hike in the scorching temperature made us postpone the adventure. After half an hour, we were in our hotel and decided to climb Sigiriya rock the next morning as the sun was still very strong in the afternoon.

Sigiriya is an ancient rock fortress situated in the Matale District. The name Sigiriya refers to a site of historical and archaeological significance dominated by a massive column of rock nearly 200 metres high. Sigiriya rock consists of an ancient citadel built by King Kashipaya during the 5th century for his new capital. The palace and the fortress complex are recognised as one of the finest examples of ancient urban planning sites of the first millennium. Considering the uniqueness of Sigiriya, UNESCO declared it a World Heritage Site in 1982.

Initially, my intention to visit this site was due to its connection with the incidents that happened during the era of The Ramayana. Legend has it that when Ravana heard about Rama's plan to attack Lanka to take Sita back from his captivity, he suspected Sita would be found by Rama's allies and hence kept shifting Sita across several locations. Ravana thought that this was the best place to keep her.

I asked the guy in the ticket office, "Why is this place not promoted as an ancient palace of Ravana too?"

Frustratingly, he had scant information about it being Ravana's palace and kept beating the bushes. He wasn't sure.

Early morning was the best time to achieve the desired results of climbing the rock. It was something more challenging in the midday sun. My senses were overwhelmed as I looked at the phenomenally huge rock so closely. It seemed as if some cliffs were hanging out on all sides, and the rock was crowned by the remains of a centuries-old palace.

With the temperature soaring even in the early hours, we began our adventure in a jovial mood. I was quite excited. The first stage of the climb started at the end of the fountain gardens where a few wide steps were easy to tread.

The idyllic series of little stairways brought us to the boulder gardens; some leaning boulders looked fabulous. Generally, I am petrified of large rocks as they tend to have large spiders and reptiles in the creeks, but the huge boulders leading to the ultimate rock were so smooth and shining that I forgot about my fears.

It was too premature as I heard the guide telling a group of visitors, who had encircled the rock, that there was a large snake resting behind it in the growing heat. Janak curiously went further to sneak behind the rock. I immediately asked her to move away and follow the passage to the rock.

It was fascinating to see many couples posing against the huge boulders. I stood in the middle of the dusty path and gazed at the top of the rock. I was hypnotised by the natural beauty of the historical monument: the top of the rock was shining with the morning sun rays, and the eastern side looked shrouded in clouds.

It was good to burn some calories, although I had no choice. I continued a bit further, but every so often I stopped, partly to rest my old bones and partly to enjoy the scenery all around. Janak and Ashok followed me comfortably.

After a few minutes, I stopped on the terrace gardens where many visitors were resting on the benches. I needed to catch my breath before the challenging climb to the mirror wall. A black and white dog, wagging its tail, was standing on a dwarf wall, probably enjoying the fresh breeze or admiring the tranquil surroundings, seemingly unaware of the loud giggles of a group from China.

As I looked up, it seemed the whole steel structure of the staircase was stitched to the rock on the eastern side. I could clearly see the light, orange-coloured mirror wall, one of the most striking features of Sigiriya rock. The first real test commenced with a series of steep narrow stairs. There were only a handful of visitors when we started, but as I looked below, a row of disciplined hikers looked scenic.

I noticed a few older people were struggling; they had underestimated the severity of the hike. A lady, with a parting in the middle of her short hair, was holding her head in both hands. She was trying to catch her breath. It looked a bit scary as she was breathing heavily.

The first hour's climb was not particularly stiff, but the trek of the steel structure seemed treacherous. The steel stairs were swirling straight up around the steel pole. The horizontal steel steps were so narrow that 2 persons side by side could not pass. It put extra pressure on me as the crowd of young men behind me was getting bigger; I could not take it easy even if I wanted. It was tough on my old knees, but I carried on climbing; for a moment, I felt as though my feet had a different owner. The banister of the spiral staircase was already getting hot by 9 am. I could not understand how people would tackle them in the middle of the day. At the top of the stairs was a little platform to catch a breath and to enjoy the mirror wall as well as the scenery.

I tried to placate my nerves by admiring the views. There were no mirrors as such, but the wall, in its prime, was so highly polished that the king could see his reflection while walking alongside it. It was made of brick masonry and covered in highly polished plaster. The wall was partly covered with verses scribbled by visitors. I could not make out anything from the faded writing. The approach and the set-up of the mirror wall were more spectacular than the wall itself; the placement of the wall on the western edge of the rock was a good work of art.

Another spiral steel staircase took us to the famous frescoes on the wall. The wall was almost entirely covered by frescoes, created during the reign of King Kashyapa. We could not see most of them as the authorities had blocked the passage to protect them from the rowdy visitors. I was in awe of the ancient paintings, though they were fading in places.

Some officials were manning the rope barriers to restrict the visitors from going beyond the specified area to protect the frescoes.

While Janak and Ashok admired the paintings, I jokingly asked the staff member, "Is there any shortcut to the top?"

"No, sir," he said while looking strangely at me.

"You have to tread a few more steps. Just take it easy."

An old man, holding a hat in his hand and listening to our conversation, smiled and said, "That would be fine, wouldn't it? The lift would be even better."

It was good to have a loud laugh after the arduous hike. Initially, I thought the steps wouldn't be as much of a battle as they were made out to be. Believe me, the steel steps' climb was a hike to remember.

As soon as the stretch of the steel staircase finished, I heaved a sigh of relief and rehydrated myself. As I looked up, my spirit began to lift. I wasn't far away from the terrace of the Lion Rock. The scenery on the last stretch before touching the mid-level terrace was mind-blowing. The view of the vast spreading forest was before my eyes. A walk, which was almost flat around the rock, gave a good view of the grandeur of the gardens below; I could have spent more time admiring nature, but the Sun God forced me to move on.

I reached the mid-level terrace, also called Lion's Paw, a little tired and disoriented. The approach to the various levels and the 'Lion's Paw' was glorious and glamorous in the end. I was really surprised that Ashok in his early seventies made it to the top with full enthusiasm. Janak took time but looked quite comfortable. After covering more than two-thirds of the total hike, we desperately needed a rest before pushing for the final assault. I realised that I hadn't got the same stamina as I used to have a few years back. My bottle of water was drained, and so was I.

This ancient palace on the top was named Sigiriya. The term Sigiriya originated from the word Sihagri, which means Lion Rock. This was designed in the form of a huge stone lion, whose feet have survived up to the present-day, but the head collapsed years ago. The legs and paws flanked the entrance to the palace. We rested our weary feet for a while before launching our final assault.

I began the ascent gingerly, but felt slightly comfortable for a few steps. As I went up the narrow steel steps towards the rock that rose out of a huge mouth of a lion, I realised how strenuous and difficult the journey was for a person like me, who was in their mid-sixties. Even my hip began to feel the pressure of climbing the small steps. But, my willpower was much stronger than my hip and knees.

The steel staircase seemed a lot longer and higher but, despite all the huffing and puffing, I scrambled to the top in rather less physical pain, though still felt breathless. Two hours in and we were, eventually, on top of the world; that's the way I felt. There were many climbers resting around a small tree at the entrance to the summit. We joined them until we caught our breath.

Few places in the world blend the achievements of mankind and the wonders of nature as perfectly as Sigiriya rock. Archaeologist H.C.P. Bell was the first archaeologist to conduct extensive research on Sigiriya.

Sigiriya site was both a palace and a fortress. The lower palaces were located behind the lavish gardens and moats which protected the citadel; the moats and wells that surrounded the lower palace were exquisitely beautiful. A mid-level terrace that included the lion gate and the mirror wall, including its frescoes, was one of the main attractions of the Rock.

The ruins of an upper palace located on the top flat of the rock seemed the most elaborate area of the Sigiriya site. The cisterns cut into the rocks indicated the plumbing and craftsmanship skills during the 5th century. Isn't it ironic that the names of the engineers or the labour that provided all these massive fortress and palaces were never mentioned anywhere, only the names of the ruling kings were flaunted all over?

After rehydrating, we set off for the ultimate viewing. As I walked past the cistern in the rock and emerged on the top, the panorama hit me like a physical assault. I was awe-struck. It brought history to life as well as a smile to my face. It was like a vast roof garden with no real produce or plants and flowers. Mother nature and the mother of engineering seemed to work so well together and complemented each other like best friends. My eyeballs gazed all around the scenery below and saw the rows of visitors walking in the gardens. There were clusters of trees all around. The entire rock was encircled by a moat. It was gloriously photogenic.

The design of the ruined palace on the top was unbeatable. The foundation of the ancient ruins of a vast palace and gardens on the huge rock terrace looked as if they were rolling off in every direction. The three- to four-brick-high foundations of the structure and the style of the King's central hall, bedrooms, and other royal rooms were kept intact. Some rooms and gardens were at a 10-15 feet drop; the lake was at a further drop of 30 feet. A large 'Throne' made from a monolith beside the lake was kept intact with the billboard stating, 'Do not sit here'. I struggled to imagine how they would have coped with daily activities and requirements at such a height.

According to mythology, I was wandering in the precinct of Ravana's palace. It provoked a sense of inquisitiveness and enthusiasm to learn more. The guides were explaining the history of the kings, the beauty of the palaces, and how they lived lavishly in the sky palaces to some groups of visitors from different countries. My eyes registered it as a Ravana citadel. I tried to imagine it in The Ramayana era when Ravana kept Sita in this palace as a prisoner. It seemed quite likely as Ravana had a grand style of living in these environments.

We roamed on the huge terrace. It offered some sweeping panoramic views at 360 degrees. As I swung my binoculars towards the west, my eyes were drawn to the highest mountain, now known as the Pidurangala Rock. It was mentioned in The Ramayana as the tallest hill which Hanuman visited in the form of a dwarf monkey and glanced into Ravana's Palace in search of Sita. I was there on a mission to visualise and analyse the viability of the Palace in The Ramayana era. Although there was no obvious evidence that Ravana ever lived there, the history and the set-up of the palace and caves around the rock certainly shed some light on his presence at some point. I could easily relate the entire region to Ravana's Citadel. The iconic Rock with the royal environment was surrounded by the fascinating green forest. It gave more weight to the view that only Ravana could have chalked out this massive set up during his regime.

My thoughts asked why the Kings in the 5th century would make this region their capital when there were many other easy options, which were implemented by different kings in later years. I could not visualise many inhabitants living around Sigiriya, and it being a capital city. There was a possibility that there were remains of a ruined Palace from The Ramayana era and that the King restructured and then dwelt on the rock. If the Kings had discovered the place as a royal site, why didn't they develop the nearby tall Pidurangala Rock too? Hence, the authenticity of Ravana's Palace on the rock held more favour in my head.

We spent around an hour at the iconic site. In terms of mythology, it was the most impressive and peculiar place I had witnessed so far.

As Janak and I were going further down, we came across a couple with their teenage daughter from Germany. I tried to communicate with a few words in German but could not do it much justice. I told them that I needed to have a grasp of the German language before I could go any further; they couldn't control their laughter. I asked them if it was their first venture thus far.

The gentleman said, "I have visited here with my girlfriend before I got married; and now we wanted our daughter to experience the same adventure before getting married. I loved this place then, and love it even more now. We shall be heading to Australia in a couple of days for a relaxing holiday."

We could not hang around for long as the sun was beaming low and showing its strength. The mythology, history, and heritage in Sri Lanka were no more potent than in Sigiriya.

Fortunately, after Lion Rock, the descending route was different, leading to a short cut to the car park. My spirits soared, but it still took longer than I thought, even though we were more relaxed on the way down.

It was a perfect setting for the end of our trek. There were many small stalls selling various kinds of soft drinks, chilled coconut water, and snacks. A few visitors were cherishing the moment in the shade.

By night, I was exhausted. A couple of capsules of paracetamol were a good substitute to massage my sore limbs, and I drifted off to a sound sleep.

Even after a good night's sleep, my legs needed warmth in the sun by the poolside. I fancied staying back a few more hours to soothe my weary joints, but the next missions to Ritigala and then to Trincomalee were playing on my mind. The aching limbs had no choice but to be satisfied with another dose of paracetamol.

TRINCOMALEE - KONESHWARAM

As we left Sigiriya for Trincomalee via Riti Gala, the blue had turned to grey above us; a respite from the heat, but the patches of sunlight remained strong. While going towards Habarana, we took a right turn to visit Riti Gala. It is believed to be one of the places where a chunk of a mountain fell when Hanuman was carrying it to save the life of Lakshmana.

We had been on the red dusty road for a while when the driver asked the only person in sight for directions to Riti Gala as he had taken a wrong turn. On a narrow road, the only sound was a distant tractor ploughing the fields. A well-maintained inquiry office was located on the left, but there was nobody around. There were trenches and dense jungle on either side, and the silence was intense; the sun's rays could not pierce through the clusters of trees.

I jokingly asked the driver, "What will happen if an elephant comes crashing out of the forest?"

"Well, take a ride on an elephant," he smirked.

Some boulders and tall trees closed in at the end of the road; a complex with a rectangular wooden office was in front of us. I could not spot any place where I could say a special chunk of the mountain was visible; it might have been in the forest further up. I expected fantastic scenery, but it was nothing more than a forest in a preserve.

TRINCOMALEE

On the map, it looked a short journey from Sigiriya to Trincomalee by road; however, we spent the best part of the day toiling through many forests and eerie stretches. As we entered Trincomalee, we were desperate for a drink. The driver stopped beside a small store where he helped the lady to extract some fresh fruit juice and mixed it with ice cream; it tasted simply out of this world. While they were busy inside the shop, I tasted some small green oval-shaped fruit that looked like a Ber-fruit in India. They were tasteless, but I kept nibbling until the driver passed me a glass of iced drink. He told me that this fruit is called Varelu, and it is very good for diabetes. He even gifted me a bag full of Varelu on my departure.

Our hotel was on a sandy beach. It was so tranquil that the silence was broken only by the roar of waves. As I gazed at the shimmering sea from the rear balcony, it looked enchanting with the waves coming fast towards the sun loungers and dying a few metres away. Listening to the birds, or rather crows, in the trees in the open garden was therapeutic.

A light siesta raised my energy level; we were ready to explore one of the most revered and famous places in the country, the Koneshwaram Temple, dedicated to Lord Shiva. It was situated on the tip of Swami Rock.

Trincomalee is one of the top 5 largest and magnificent natural harbours in the world. Sri Lanka's longest river, the Mahaweli, springs from the central hills and enters the sea here at Mutur, south of Circular Bay. It has served as a major maritime seaport in the international trading history of the island. The port switched hands back and forth among the Portuguese, Dutch, French, and British until 1795.

Given that Sri Lanka has such a rich cricketing pedigree, I expected to see many men playing the game on every beach and in every park, but on the contrary, there was no sign of cricket or the locals on the beaches. It was completely a tourist destination with hotels all along the sea; the local traffic was rather sparse.

We drove past a park where some deer were resting lethargically under the tree. Just a few hundred metres away from the sea was the main entrance gate of Fort Frederick, which was part of Swami Rock; it looked unappealing. As we went up the hill, the temple on the edge of the rock and a few boats in the sea offered stupendous views. It was not only spiritually enchanting but also breathtakingly beautiful; some dark grey massive rocks on the right, and Lord Shiva's huge statue bang in the heart of a courtyard on the way to the shrine looked awe-inspiring.

There was a big gap between the huge rocks in the shape of 'V' called Ravana Vettu – meaning Ravana cleft or Ravana-cut. It is believed that King Ravana and his mother had worshipped Shiva at the shrine. When his mother was in ill health, he wanted to remove the temple of Koneshwaram to his palace. Ravana performed penance for a Shiva Lingam but upon receiving no response, he became angry. As Ravana was heaving the entire mountain, he was pummelled by Shiva. Ravana, in rage, pulled out his sword and inflicted a huge cut in the hill.

The main temple itself looked magnificent with towering gopuras carved in Dravidian style. As we entered the temple premises, the rich colour scheme, frescoes, and murals depicted the mythical tales on the walls all around; they were supported by some deities with ornate outfits enshrined in a small but decorated sanctuary in the right corner. It appealed to the eye at the first instance.

The Swami Rock's ancient history is more mystery and sometimes highly debatable. The Koneshwaram temple stands on the eastern promontory of Trincomalee; it is mentioned in both The Ramayana and Mahabharata. An underwater explorer, De Queiroz, the Portuguese historian, not only described the exact location of the shrine but also described it as the 'Rome of the Orient' which pilgrims frequented more than Rameshwaram or the Jagannath temples in Puri in India.

Many devotees, coincidentally staying in our hotel, from South India, made up the majority of the pilgrims; the priest was paying more attention to them for the evening aarti as they were appropriately dressed; women wore saris and men wore no shirts. As the priests began to chant mantras and rang the bells simultaneously, we became a part of it by threading our way through the local devotees. The whole place came alive with drumming and sounds of bells all around. The Shiva Lingam was enthroned in a small room around 10 metres away; we stood and enjoyed the ambience of the evening aarti. As I pointed my camera towards the Lingam, the priest came up and asked me to switch it off.

I decided to come back the next day for the morning aarti. On the way back, near the tall statue of Shiva, we met a few Buddhist monks marching towards the shrine in a queue. I asked a couple of them to join us for a photo session beside the deity; they had come from Cambodia.

Early in the morning, as I inched past the same priest who had denied me photography last night, he still looked angry. I registered a poorly concealed dismay as I had a camera around my neck, but I was there to pay my obeisance. I was soaking in the luxury of spirituality. Another regular devotee, a temple committee member too, was engrossed in his daily orientation. I asked him about the importance of the place. He advised me to buy a book that explained everything about the temple's history. As I was paying for it, I realised it was written in Tamil; I did not want to change my mind but thought about donating it to the Hindu temple in Newcastle where many Tamils pay their obeisance.

I asked him if I could take some photos of the murals on the walls. He not only allowed it but also took us to the small shrine opposite the main temple, which they open only at the time of puja. The mystique of the complex was the Ravan's statue that was carved out of the black granite. It was enshrined under the tree on the edge of the rock facing the main temple denoting his devotion towards Lord Shiva. The same gentleman even arranged our lift in the official vehicle to the car park. As dusk gently turned into night, there was nothing much to do in the area; early night, a rare phenomenon, was a bliss.

TALAIMANNAR - KOTESHWARAM

Before we left the hotel, I felt delighted that I would witness the seashore of Talaimannar where Lord Rama, together with his forces, first set foot on the land of Lanka. As we left Trincomalee behind, the vista on either side of the road kept me occupied; the cows were grazing on the grass in hilly fields. A thick cluster of trees in the background at regular intervals reminded me of travelling in the north of England, from Hexham to Carlisle.

I asked the driver to take a detour to Madhu, a remote village where the Church of 'Our Lady of Madhu' is situated.

I said to him, "Let's have the blessings of Jesus, too."

"Sure," he said with a smile, as he was a Christian himself.

He looked elated. He explained, "The church is around 8 kilometres from the main road that leads to Mannar. We should be there in 3 hours. You will enjoy one of the best sceneries of Sri Lanka."

He took a short cut to the church. But the dusty red road seemed like a wrong choice as the needle on the speedometer could not cross the 30 km mark. Upon entering the church complex, it was a mind-blowing sight. An enormous light blue building spread out in 3 directions; its surroundings extended for 5 kilometres around the church.

The shrine of Our Lady of Madhu is a Roman Catholic Marian church in Mannar District. With a history of over 400 years, it is situated in the middle of the jungle, and the shrine acts as a centre of pilgrimage and worship for the Sri Lankan Catholics.

The ambience was tranquil and peaceful throughout the premises. It was supposed to be the biggest church in Sri Lanka. The Pope had made a visit to the place in 2015, and the walls in the office were decorated with photographs of the Pope with various dignitaries. Inside the church, the statue depicting Mother Mary holding the infant Jesus is centuries-old and is believed to have healing powers. In fact, it was a very charming experience to be there.

The town of Mannar was around 25 miles from the main gate of Madhu. Just before reaching Mannar city, the driver took a right turn to visit an ancient Shiva temple, Koteshwaram. A sense of excitement ran through my body, and my attention was diverted towards the spiritual aura again.

The sun was scorching hot as we reached the temple car park, but that did not bother me. As I came out of the car, my first impression led to some disappointment, which did not change when the visit was over. The beauty of the main structure and the architecture on the gopuram was eye-catching. It was situated in a secluded corner. There was no other vehicle parked in the vicinity of the temple, which indicated that we had arrived during closing hours.

There was no one in the small office but soon, an attendant who could not speak a word of English arrived. He told the driver in Sinhalese to ask us to remove our shirts and shoes before entering the shrine. The floor was red hot; I could easily warm up the pizza on the tiles. I hopped towards the shaded area.

The entire complex looked to be under renovation, and the scaffolding spoiled the beauty of the premises. Even the main sanctum outside the shrine and the vast hall around it had been demolished. Some half-erected cement pillars were the centre of attraction. All the small shrines on both sides of the vicinity were being demolished. But it was not all doom and gloom; the glory of the temple had not been lost, and I could visualise the grandeur of the complex after completion.

I concentrated on the spiritual side, as this temple is of great importance. Legend has it that the temple was built by Ravan's father-in-law, as he was a great devotee of Shiva. Somehow, Rama had visited the place at some point during his stay in Lanka. We paid our obeisance in front of the main shrine and asked for pardon.

TALAIMANNAR

The fishing town of Talaimannar did not look very big, but the traffic indicated that everyone had some sort of daily chores to do. The roads in every direction were full of two-wheelers.

In fact, I did not even notice when we had crossed the city and reached the shore of the sea which connected Rama Setu to Dhanush Kodi in India. We were beside the watchtower near the main pier that was under the jurisdiction of the Sri Lankan navy. While the driver went to ask about exploring the place, we walked towards the pier but were not allowed to stroll on it. The pier was not in a healthy state, and close photography was prohibited around the Navy-controlled sites. It was a place of arrival and departure for ferries in the recent past. The historical photographs of the ferry service to Dhanush Kodi and the bustling pier in her heyday were posted on the billboard beside the pier entrance. A lighthouse appeared to be the tallest building in the area, standing across the boundary wall at less than a hundred metres away.

After a few minutes' strolling in the midday heat, the driver took us across the pier, towards the lighthouse. On the way, we crossed the railway track and the newly renovated railway station of Talaimannar, the last main station on the west coast.

We walked past a maze of dusty paths and semi-permanent huts. Eventually, we were on the shore that I had long dreamt of witnessing. It was dotted with fishing boats; some moored partly in the waters and others scattered on the sand. Many birds were flying low over the waters, probably searching for their prey; a stray dog was chasing the birds on the wet sand. Everyone looked busy in their daily chores. Some women were busy unloading the plastic containers of fresh fish, while some men were pulling the dinghy boats out from the shallow waters. A group of men stood in the shade whispering and smiling.

The acrid and foul smell of rotten fish hung in the air, though it was not so strong in the hot sun. Even with all these activities going on, the atmosphere was filled with silence. I did not hear anyone talking; the only sound was from the birds flapping their feathers, and even the dogs were walking lethargically in the hot sand.

What a contrast; the sight of 2 towns and seas joining the Rama Setu. Dhanush Kodi in India was a ghost town, only busy with many tourists and beautiful clean beaches, whereas Talaimannar in Sri Lanka, the slower-paced one, had an active fishing community but no apparent visitors, even though it has better infrastructure, including the railway station.

A wide smile broke out on my face, and my heart soared. This was the ultimate place that I had wanted to visit since I found out from a news channel that you could witness the Rama Setu in the sea from the Sri Lankan side. In fact, before the destruction by a cyclone in December 1964, it was the terminus of a ferry service to India. It was part of the Indo-Lankan railway service, where passengers were ferried between Talaimannar and Dhanush Kodi on Rameshwaram Island in India. The *pier that is now under Naval control was a railway track. The maps of the routes and services in that period were clearly illustrated on the board just before the entrance to the pier.*

The eighteen-kilometre-long Rama Setu is a series of small sandbanks and corals connecting the southern tip of India at Dhanush Kodi to Talaimannar in the northwest of Sri Lanka. For mythology and history enthusiasts, it would be riveting to walk on the sandbanks; also, for Hindu pilgrims, it would be the unique experience of seeing the largely undiscovered footprints of The Ramayana. Hence, I wanted to fulfil my heartfelt desire to witness the Rama Setu by hook or by crook.

I could feel the hot sand beneath my feet and sandals, yet my mind was wandering elsewhere. I restlessly gazed at the blue sea and wandered in the sweltering heat while the driver was busy persuading the fishermen for a trip to the desired spot, around 5 kilometres out from the shore. A nod of approval was given by the fishermen. The driver had played a key role in organising the hiring of the boat.

Most of the fishermen looked at us with curiosity; some women whispered to each other and smiled. They spoke no English, but we were made to feel welcome. As I walked towards the boat, for a split second, I thought it could be quite perilous getting into the sea without any security in an unofficial boat, when no one in our families knew that we were venturing out on the sea. But there was no other option that could provide a substitute for going out there. Despite my worries, I felt wonderfully exhilarated, strolling along the sea on the ground where Lord Rama and his forces once walked.

I could count on the fingers of one hand the times I have gone out in a boat on the sea, let alone on an unauthorised dinghy boat. But this time, my mind followed what my heart said, "Leave it to Lord Rama; you must go, Prabhu."

My inner child was itching, but in fact, I did not have a clue what I was going to witness and what joy the sight would unleash in the middle of the sea. This trip was not only to admire the atmosphere but also the religious significance of the place. It was the heart and soul of the entire itinerary.

It took a good few minutes to get into the motorboat as there was no jetty; a plastic container was used for a platform. The fishing boat was not designed to take passengers, so Janak and Indu adjusted themselves on the plastic crates. Ashok and I rested against the back wall of the boat. I noticed a circle of small silver fish which darted about, showing their skills in triple somersaults. The roar of the engine made them disappear into the blue waters.

As we sailed over the quiet expanse of the waters, the sun was shining across the sea, which looked as if it were embossed by the small waves. It all seemed perversely idyllic, with 3 boatmen laughing at us as we were unable to hold onto the side of the boat. I felt as though I were on the deck of a small ship cresting the waves on a special mission. I noticed a common tern riding a floating log and looking in our direction, probably keeping an eye on the new entrants into the sea.

As my confidence in the water grew, possibly due to the spiritual inclination, I had strange heavenly feelings. The young boatmen were laughing so cheerfully that any misgivings evaporated in the sea air. I tried to take some photographs in the fast-moving boat, but very few snaps exhibited what I wanted to capture in the frame. A boatman asked me in sign language if he could turn up the throttle. I showed my 'thumbs up'.

As the boat was speeding up, all I could hear was the slosh of water. I was growing more intrigued about how they would find the right place to stop without any radar or compass. But they were spot on; they knew their job very well. I could not believe my luck. Rama Setu came into view as they halted. We fell silent, including the boat engine. I was exactly at the place where once Lord Rama and his allies walked; this really was the place of dreams. A wave of divinity ran through my entire body. I felt goose pimples.

This was the most jubilant moment of my travelling life. We were alone, and solitude suited us to the hilt. We wanted to explore the Rama Setu in our own time as it was the unique place in the entire journey of The Ramayana sites.

The boatmen could not speak English at all, but again asked me with sign language if we'd feel comfortable jumping off the boat to wade in the shallow water. Andha Kya mange, do Aankhen? – It was like 2 eyes being offered to a blind man. It was hard to control my excitement; it added a wonderful dimension to what was already a unique trip. I had never dreamt of going out 5 kilometres into the sea and leaving the boat to walk in the water to witness the most venerated Setu among Hindus.

The divine powers and the inner quest brought me to this unique revered site. There was emptiness on the horizon, yet it gave me wonderful feelings to gaze around the sea; it was simply fantastic. Based on satellite studies by NASA, Rama Setu is the bridge that Hanuman and his associates built for Rama to cross over to Lanka.

In my mind's eye, I had envisaged something like this, as we have been watching and listening to many stories related to The Ramayana. It surpassed all expectations. It was a part of Rama Setu where our boat was moored. I realised that the sea was so shallow that the boat was resting on the submerged sand bank. It was glorious in its incongruity. The remnants of the Setu were evident in the knee-high water. It seemed almost like a meeting between Dhanush Kodi and Talaimannar. It was hard to believe that we were still in Sri Lanka. I could visualise a good swimmer easily moving from one shoal to another and reaching India in a matter of a few hours.

Apart from the sound of our excitement, it was perfectly silent, with not a breath of wind. I was in a state of bliss. I waddled up and down for a few seconds but could not wait to feel the water any longer. Ashok and I stepped out into the sea. I felt that only by being there was it possible to get the real feelings and full appreciation of this magnificent site. Seeing the rising sand in the clear water while walking gave me true sensations of spirituality. I absorbed the pleasure and spiritual contentment in equal measures. I felt curiously close to its history and nature. It revealed yet another layer of the past, the most important one.

These sandbanks lie less than a foot underwater in many places and might only have been submerged as recently as 1480, according to temple records from Rameshwaram in India. The unique curvature underwater indicated the bridge to be man-made. The splendour of the site was not visible, but the triumph and the extra layer of discovery were evident.

Janak's eyes were immediately drawn to the rising sand in the shallow water. She was itching to witness the feel of the place. With the help of the boatmen, she tumbled into the sea while trying to hold onto the rope attached to the boat. A look of delight was clearly written on her face. Indu was equally enjoying the view from the boat. Janak walked on the sand looking radiant from the excitement of witnessing The Ramayana site. She was scooping the water in both hands and showing the floating grains of sand. We all had childlike feelings in the middle of the sea. I splashed water in the air and tried to catch the rising sand in the water. We were not the only ones buzzing; the boatmen were relishing our activities too. They were laughing loudly while saying something in Sinhalese. They might have brought many other pilgrims to this place but wouldn't have seen such a maniacal bunch before.

Waddling in the water that had sand and Setu beneath my feet was one of the best spiritual moments of my life. I was encapsulated in the sacred waters and felt blessed. It surpassed all my preconceptions. I felt I was there as a devotee on a pilgrimage rather than as a writer.

For a couple of minutes, I closed my eyes and tried to envisage the scene of Lord Rama crossing the bridge, but I did not have the courage to look directly into the eyes of Gods. I was not accustomed to such vibrations. A fearful thought jumped out of my heart. I took a few steps beside the boat, scrunched my eyes shut, braced myself, and then silently prayed and paid obeisance in my heart. As I asked for forgiveness, an inspirational chanting came from my lips – Jai Sri Rama – victory to Lord Rama.

The whole experience left a profound spiritual effect on me. I didn't feel like leaving the place, but all good things come to an end. As we left, I kept looking back at the waters as if I was departing from God's own abode. I took blessings and his permission to leave but promised to come back soon.

Heading back to the beach, I had both good and bad feelings. Although I had experienced the thrill of seeing the place, I wasn't fully satisfied because we had rushed through the trip. It was more annoying when I found out that after a couple of miles, there was a small island on the Setu where we could have landed and spent a longer time. "Well, there is always another time," I thought.

Everyone on the seashore cheered us as we left the boat. I dodged some litter on the sand and went inside the temporary canopy where a few women were sorting out the fresh load of fish. I knew they wouldn't understand my language, but I thanked them for allowing their men to take us on a trip when it was their busy time. They understood the universal language and thanked back with folded hands and a smile.

As I paid the agreed amount and an extra tip out of my wet pocket, the notes were sticking together. The main guy separated the notes and wafted them in the air to dry them off. One man said something in their language; they all burst into loud laughter. The expressions on their faces showed great satisfaction.

The driver of our car, along with some fishermen, waited for us under the temporary canopy. He looked very happy to see that we were fully satisfied with our journeys. I shook his hand and heartily thanked him for his efforts.

This was the jewel in the crown of my tour; history, myth, and legend were embedded in these waters. My regret at not staying longer on the Rama Setu in the sea will linger on until I go back again. Yet, if I never come back here again, I could still die peacefully.

JAFFNA

It took around 4 hours to drive the 150 kilometres from Talaimannar to Jaffna. For a quarter of a century, this route was largely out of bounds for tourists. The civil war came to a head in 1983 when the Liberation Tigers of Tamil Eelam - LTTE - killed dozens of Sri Lankan soldiers. Many troops in various camps could be seen in several places, which meant that it was now safe and comfortable to travel to the northernmost city of Sri Lanka. Although the coastal road was an unconventional route, the newly built highway A32 was very smooth and picturesque.

The long drive seemed to go on forever. Often, the newly laid railway track ran parallel to the road. It would have been a great experience to drive alongside the train, but we did not come across anyone on the entire route. As we were passing through many war-torn places, the driver showed us some battle sites and their significance.

After a while, Dushan asked me, "Sir, do you wish to take a snap of the newly built bridge?"

I was not sure whether he really wanted me to take a photograph as he had been suggesting opportunities at many picturesque places, or if he wanted me to stay awake as I was sitting next to him. He might have noticed my head falling a few times as I felt like having a snooze. Anyhow, the sight was pleasing to the eye; many other people were gazing around and clicking their cameras too. It looked as if lots of roads and bridges on the way to Jaffna have been painstakingly rebuilt.

It was a good omen that we were able to visit the Hanuman shrine on the way to the hotel in Jaffna. As the setting sun began to dip fast behind the residential buildings, the sky was almost losing its red-orange lustre. All day travelling had caused a slightly sore head, but a couple of paracetamol capsules soon took care of it.

Next morning, there was no hanging about. First, we called at Neela Wari well. It was the place where Lord Rama shot an arrow at the ground to obtain water and assuage the thirst of his forces upon reaching Lanka. It was a small historical place with an unexciting appearance. It seemed that only a few tourists visit the site. The prime attraction, Neela Wari well, was at the precise point where the arrow had pierced the ground. The well was right in the middle of the complex.

It is believed that the well was somehow connected directly to the sea; anything that went in never came back. The blue water didn't look drinkable. The well was surrounded by a short boundary wall with steel railings to protect anyone from leaning over too far. The raised passageway along the wall was a convenient place to get a good view of the site. The borderless gateway to the well from the rear side looked dangerous, but there were some security guards at the entry gate who also wandered around the complex.

Soon after, we proceeded to the Naguleshwarm Temple in Keerimalai. This northernmost temple at the edge of the ocean is dedicated to Lord Shiva. Parts of the temple had to be removed after bomb damage, but the huge shrine and the passages around the inner sanctum were intact. They were highly decorated with murals of various Gods and goddesses and contained statues of the deities, which added to the spirituality of the place.

A priest with a broad smile on his face came over and asked, "Where are you from?"

"I am a Punjabi from India but have resided in England for over 40 years."

He looked baffled. He gestured towards his head and asked hesitantly, "Where is your turban?"

"Mostly Sikhs wear turbans. Not everyone living in Punjab is Sikh. I am a Hindu Brahmin."

"Okay! Okay," he felt awkward and pretended he understood it all.

For a split second, I was bemused as the manager of the hotel had asked me the same question in the morning. Light-heartedly, I had told him, "Why do I need a turban when I have no hair?"

I realised that for over a quarter of a century, the people of northern Sri Lanka have had little contact with the outside world; therefore, their inquisitiveness was only natural. The presumption that all Punjabis wear a turban still occasionally does the rounds in my head. It cements my viewpoint that travelling is the best method of widening your horizon.

The driver could not find the location of the hot springs in Keerimalai, so we decided to come back to the hotel for lunch and a bit of rest. En route, he paused at the juice parlour so that we could quench our thirst. We unanimously ordered some Shakanjavi, which is water infused with fresh lemons and some black salt and pepper. It was so refreshing that I wanted another glass, but a long queue prompted me to move on.

It did not look like a war-torn city. Everyone seemed to be doing well for themselves. I did not feel as if I was in Sri Lanka. It was like wandering around a city in southern India.

Foreign tourists were a novelty in the region, but a warm welcome came our way at every place we stopped. Northern Sri Lanka has been an unconventional tourist destination, but for the visitors from South India, it has become the place to witness the damage caused by the war. Many residential properties, churches, and just about every government building were bombarded and gutted by fire. The scars of war were reminders of the recent past and could be seen in every direction. Near the National Park was a shell of a church standing by the roadside. There wasn't much left in the church, but whatever had survived depicted the tale of its glorious past. Even the trees weren't spared. Some headless palm trees stood in the open fields. The bombardment on nature, which had nothing to do with any community, saddened me the most.

After a light lunch, Ashok and Indu went to their room for a power nap, but Janak and I decided to explore the iconic railway station of Jaffna. I could hear the hoarse whistling of the engine in the early morning as our hotel was just next to it. It was the northernmost railway station of Sri Lanka. The elevation of the building bore the signature of colonial times and looked very impressive. It clearly exhibited the British presence in the past. The newly renovated platforms with electronic signboards and clean tracks looked marvellously pristine.

There were no trains on the tracks, but we did come across a solitary passenger. A European was waiting for the train even though it was still over 4 hours away. I asked a member of the railway staff who was sitting on a wooden box near the exit about the timings of the trains. He could not understand English or Hindi but raised 4 fingers; thank God he did not show one or 2!

Jaffna was best known for being the epicentre of the civil war, but now it has a strong attraction for tourists. It has many historical and striking places to boast about. The remnants of the British era were apparent, and the place could not shrug off its colonial past. The Jaffna Library building was a perfect example, probably the best, of monuments built during the British occupation. The largest library in Asia was burnt down by the Sri Lankan rebels on June 1, 1981. With the help of many foreign governments, it was restored to its original glory, though the irreparable loss of books was evident. The statue of Saraswati – the

Goddess of knowledge and wisdom – in the front courtyard magnified its significance.

The most impressive and amazing custom was practiced there. We had to remove our shoes at the reception. There was a suitable counter for depositing shoes and motorbike helmets. As they say, "Coming events cast their shadows before;" it felt wonderful entering the educational institution barefoot. I asked the receptionist if we could meet the Chief Librarian to express our gratitude as she was managing such a fabulous establishment.

The Chief Librarian was busy with her routine work during the hours of closure, but she came up and greeted us with an open heart. She was a very pleasant and cordial woman who took us to her small office and made us feel comfortable.

After exchanging pleasantries and briefly touching on the horrific incidents during the war, she explained to us, "We have lost an enormous number of books including some great encyclopaedias and many rare collections of books. Some foreign governments are helping to build up the stock. France and China have donated many books, but most of them are in their own language."

I could feel the pain in her voice. She was quite happy to let me take her photograph along with Janak and Indu. She also assured me that she would be glad to grace the library with my book when it is published.

As we were coming back to the reception, I spotted a picture of Thiruvalluvar, the great poet from Tamil Nadu in India. It was delightfully arranged on a small bench against the wall, with incense sticks spreading their fragrance all around. It was wonderful to witness the respect showered upon the intellectuals of the literary world. The librarian seemed bemused and surprised that I recognised the poet at once.

She arranged a tour of the library, even though it was before the opening time. There was a special 'Indian Corner' room where they kept books donated by India. Most of them were written in Tamil or English. Extreme care had been given to the design of the building. The rooms had been constructed to join the long corridors and junctions. It felt quite cool even during the warm day. The entire stock of newspapers was wiped out in the fire, but they showed some newspapers and periodicals that had been acquired since 1981.

The main lobby displayed many photographs of ruined sections of the library. They were heart-rending moments. Although I was pleased to witness the great institution restored to its original glory and managed by an able librarian, I felt sad to see the irreparable loss incurred by the destruction of the books.

Just behind the Library, on the western lagoon, the second biggest fort of Sri Lanka (the first being the Galle Fort) was located, but I postponed my visit to the place as I was still in a sombre mood.

After visiting another notable Hindu monument, the large Nallur Kandaswamy Temple, dedicated to Shiva, the driver decided to take us to the hot springs in Keerimalai, which he could not find in the morning.

The sun was plunging below the rooftops; the light was fading fast, but the car's accelerator was pressed down to the floor. The driver was determined to reach the destination in daylight.

We were back at the same spot near the Naguleshwaram Temple, hugging the northern shore of the peninsula. The Keerimalai hot springs were in a desolate area, tucked behind a few religious dwellings. There wasn't a human voice to be heard; the silence was eerie in the late evening.

The seafront beyond the pool was covered in darkness; only a slight shine on the sea drew attention to its existence. The hot springs were contained in a rectangular concrete pool surrounded by a small wall. The stone steps surrounding the water tank were an architectural landmark.

As we went further, there was no sound of any kind, but I could see the heads of a couple of men swimming around in the still water. I thought that they were local guys as their workbags were placed near the far corner. To get the real feel of the water, Janak ventured out to fulfil her wish of washing her face with the holy spring water. She probably sensed that the hot spring had healing properties.

As it was getting very dark, we decided not to stroll around the beach. We had to speak loudly to enable us to follow each other to the car park, but it was worth the effort.

The next morning brought a surprise: I spotted 6 or 7 Sri Lankan cricket coaches in the hotel lobby. Being a lover of sport, especially cricket, I could not contain myself.

I went to them and asked, "Are you playing for the nation?"

"No, we are national coaches," said one of them.

"Excellent."

"We are judging some players' abilities and coaching them in colleges and other institutions. There isn't much cricket played in this part of the country. It is mostly played in the south."

After a brief two-day stay, I felt sad to say goodbye to Jaffna. I wanted to explore the Island of Kayts and the Naag Deepa temple on Nainativu Island. It is believed that the surrounding ocean is where the Chief-serpent, Surasa, challenged Hanuman before entering Lanka. The area was so strongly reminiscent of its past that it created a compelling reason to visit soon.

There were many beautiful views for me to appreciate. I was so impressed with the charisma of the Tal trees dotted in the green fields that I asked the driver to stop the car to get a closer look at them. He immediately screeched to a halt on the roadside near the ubiquitous Tal tree. I got out of the car to admire the beauty of the tree. It wasn't very tall, but the massive spiky leaves in a symmetrical design clustered on the top looked enchanting.

Just beside the tree was a house where a lady in a printed sari was hanging her washing on an overused wooden bed outside the house. Her young son was trying to pass her the wet clothes. The driver suggested to me that I should give the child a set of stationery and a packet of sweets which I was carrying with me to donate. As I handed out some extra sweets, the gratitude on the child's face was phenomenal.

It would have been a dull, long, and tiresome journey if the driver had not kept us engaged with the tales of some incidents that had taken place during the war. They were very engrossing. They were all about the gruesome history of killing and bombings.

He paused again at a vast complex where a metal statue of an army officer on a small platform was set up; a burnt-out army tank nearby in a well-maintained garden looked mysterious. Apparently, the graceful statue was of a soldier who had blown up more than a hundred Liberation Tamil Tigers of Eelam along with their tank – on show – by suicidal bombs attached to his body.

This eye-catching site was next to the Elephant Pass railway station. It seemed as if the beautiful surroundings and the landscape were created especially for travellers to halt and admire the place. A couple of shops in the complex sold various snacks, souvenirs, and literature about the events of the war. I could not leave without buying something to support the local shopkeeper. A small rectangular, colourful basket made from Tal tree bark caught my eye.

We felt peckish by the time we reached Anuradhapura. The heat was at its height. Ashok and I had to walk over half a kilometre to find the suitable restaurant-cum-bakery. It was full of upmarket customers, a sign of good food. A yellow and white uniformed attendant behind the counter asked us to come to the front of the queue. She probably noticed us as being different or heard my belly rumbling. The menu bore no specific vegetable choices, but the spring rolls filled with paneer and wrapped roti looked appetising. Believe me, both items were so tasty that I could have eaten many more; the food kept me busy until we reached the Bodh Tree complex car park.

The stop at Sri Maha Bodhi Tree temple was a must-see destination. It was the equivalent of going to Rome and visiting the Vatican. Sri Bodhi Tree is a sacred tree in Mahamewna Gardens, Anuradhapura. It is said to have grown from a branch of the historical Sri Maha Bodhi at Bodh Gaya in India, under which Siddhartha Gautama attained Enlightenment and became known as Buddha. Buddhists view the Bodhi Tree as a symbol of Enlightenment. Even today, they continue to meditate under it.

The gravel and the path were hot to walk on. We spent some time in the temple hall. There was a healing atmosphere all around.

Most of the journey from Anuradhapura to Negombo was undertaken in near silence. My bottom was sore after almost a full day's travel.

www.ingramcontent.com/pod-product-compliance
Lightning Source LLC
LaVergne TN
LVHW021138160826
845679LV00023B/1955

9798895448991